THE
KEEPING
POWER
OF GOD

THE KEEPING POWER OF GOD

by HERBERT LOCKYER

Thomas Nelson Publishers
Nashville

Published in Nashville, Tennessee, by Thomas Nelson, Inc., Publishers and distributed in Canada by Lawson Falle, Ltd., Cambridge, Ontario.

Printed in the United States of America.

Old Testament Scripture quotations (except the Psalms) are from The King James Version of the Bible.

Scripture quotations from the New Testament and Psalms are from the New King James Bible–New Testament. Copyright © 1979, Thomas Nelson, Inc., Publishers.

Library of Congress Cataloging in Publication Data

Lockyer, Herbert.
    The keeping power of God.

    1. Christian life—1960-   I. Title.
BV4501.2.L64   248.4   81-14140
ISBN 0-8407-5252-0   AACR2

CONTENTS

PREFACE

What momentous days these are to be alive! How true are the lines:

We are living, we are dwelling,
In a grand and awful time.
In an age on ages telling,
To be living is sublime.

But sublimity of living can be ours only as we live in the orbit of God's will and purpose and daily experience His saving and keeping power. National and international events, heavy with prophetic significance, indicate that Christ's promised return may not be far distant. While on earth, He described signs foreshadowing His glorious appearing, and concluded His forecast of the future by saying, " 'When these things begin to happen *look up* and *lift up* your heads, because your redemption draws near' " (Luke 21:20–28, italics added). The word *begin* is most arrestive, for we are living in an age when what Christ predicted is *beginning* to come to pass.

The question of paramount importance is, are we living and laboring in the light of this most blessed event?

7

What impact is such a belief having upon our behavior? Referring to the day of our Lord's appearing, Peter asked, ". . . what manner of persons ought you to be in holy conduct and godliness . . . ?" (2 Pet. 3:11–18).

The meditations in the following chapters were prayerfully designed to guide saints in ways of translating beliefs into behavior, of having lives pleasing to the Lord and ready to hail His glorious appearing. The keeping power of God enables us thus to be faithful. To this end, may He be pleased to bless and use this volume as it travels far and wide.

Herbert Lockyer
Fall 1981

Chapter 1

VICTIM OR VICTOR—WHICH?

The terrible sufferings heaped upon our blessed Lord mark Him out as a victim. He was a victim of hate, shame, and cruelty. Think of the gruesome descriptions Isaiah foretold of Jesus: "I gave my back to the smiters, and my cheeks to them that plucked off the hair: I hid not my face from shame and spitting" (Is. 50:6) and ". . . his visage was so marred more than any man, and his form more than the sons of men" (Is. 52:14). The literal rendering of this last verse is more heart-moving still: "So marred from the form of man was His aspect that His appearance was not that of a son of man." His face and form were battered beyond human recognition (see Matt. 26:67,68; 27:27–30). Who, then, does Isaiah portray in his Calvary prediction but Him who would be "wounded for our transgressions, . . . bruised for our iniquities . . ." (Is. 53:5)?

What must not be forgotten, however, is the fact that Jesus was a willing victim, for His life was not taken but given. Underscore the phrase, *I gave my back* to the smiters. . . ." Then think of His own statements in respect to His voluntary surrender: ". . . I lay down My life for the sheep . . . I lay down My life that I may take it again . . . I lay it down of Myself. I have power to lay

9

it down, and I have power to take it again" (John 10: 15–18).

In His shame, suffering, and sacrifice, Christ voluntarily laid down His life, and in His resurrection He took His life up again. "Greater love has no one than this, that he lay down his life for His friends" (John 15:13). The glory of the gospel is that Jesus willingly died for His enemies. He was not forced or dragged to His cross, but led. He did not climb those bloody steps at Calvary against His will, nor was He compelled to go there by a stronger power. Had He wished, He could have smitten all His crucifiers with one breath, but He allowed Himself to be afflicted.

What amazing grace! What truth sublime! He was not driven to His cross, but drawn to it by the love of God for a lost world. This voluntary, as well as vicarious, sacrifice inspired His disciples to emulate His example, ". . . He laid down His life for us. And we ought to lay down our lives for the brethren" (1 John 3:16). "Lord . . . I will lay down my life for Your sake" (John 13:37,38).

Jesus was not only a *victim* of cruel crucifixion but also a *victor* over an awful death. As He died, His last triumphant words were "It is finished!" (John 19:30). By dying, He slew death. As the ancients were wont to say, He trampled death by death! He destroyed the Devil's power in respect to death (see Heb. 2:14–18; 1 John 3:8). In His resurrection He became "a Victor o'er the dark domain, and He lives forever with His saints to reign." Referring to a time when his past life was outside of Christ, Paul could write, ". . . who loved me and *gave Himself* for me" (Gal. 2:20, italics added).

How blessed we are if we have received Him as our victorious substitute who died in our place. He tasted death for every man. Actually the plural is used in Hebrews 2:9—*deaths*. It is beyond our finite minds to comprehend the stupendous truth that *all* deaths were rolled into *one* death, namely, the death of Christ on the cross. C. H. Spurgeon said on one occasion that all his theology could be compressed into four words: *He died for me!*

Look at Paul's declaration again: ". . . the Son of God, who loved me and gave Himself for me" (Gal. 2:20). It begins with the *Son of God* and ends with *me*. What extreme contrasts are presented by the apostle, and nothing but the cross can bring us together and make us one:

> *My need and Thy great fulness meet,*
> *And I have all in Thee.*

We are apt to forget that Golgotha was in a garden. We must not allow the cross to obliterate the garden. The combination implies that God can make us fruitful even in the land of affliction.

Christ's death and burial in a garden may be the basis for adorning graves with flowers. The blooming flowers around His cross and tomb were prophetic, floral heralds of His resurrection. So as it may appear gruesome and contradictory for blood to be dripping from Christ's wounds in such a beautiful spot, does it seem as if the garden of your life is being spoiled by some crimson-dyed, ugly-shaped cross? May your eyes be opened to discover that your cross is adding to the fragrance of your garden! Suffering often produces flowers of richer hues.

For the Savior, His outpoured blood in a garden implied joy, victory, compensation in a glorious harvest of souls, and the earnest of Paradise, with its tree of life and twelve manner of fruits (see Rev. 22:2). If your life has been emptied of its self-glory, independence, ambition, will, wisdom, and success and you find yourself rejected, despised, unwanted in the world, even by those from whom you expected sympathy, think of Jesus who died in a garden. As His tomb was in a garden, so bury your self-reputation deep in His grave, then go out bearing the aroma of the garden of resurrection, always rejoicing in the glorious news that He who died to save you from the guilt and penalty of sin is alive forevermore to keep you daily from the power of sin.

In the light of this truth, the apostle Peter said,

> Blessed be the God and Father of our Lord Jesus Christ, who according to His abundant mercy has begotten us again to a living hope by the resurrection of Jesus Christ from the dead, to an inheritance incorruptible and undefiled and that does not fade away, reserved in heaven for you" (1 Pet. 1:3,4).

Note here a theme as old as the Scriptures themselves: His abundant mercy. God's mercy is without beginning and without end. It is His mercy which causes us to be born anew and to wait in "living hope" for the coming of the Lord.

But did you know that it is the same mercy which *saves* as that which *keeps?* From time to time you will meet those who will insist without compromise that they are saved by God's mercy. But they have not yet realized that they are kept by God's mercy as well. For His abundant mercy enables us to be ". . . *kept by the power of God* through faith for salvation ready to be revealed in the last time (1 Pet. 1:5, italics added).

Did Jesus not say, ". . . Those whom you gave Me I have kept . . ."? (John 17:12). We are in a battle with Satan who wants us to fall victim to his allurements. But rejoice as we consider together the keeping power of God which is able to give us victory through Jesus Christ our Lord!

Chapter 2

PUBLIC ENEMY NO. 1

"They overcame him [Satan] by the blood of the Lamb and by the word of their testimony, and they did not love their lives to the death" (Rev. 12:11).

This apocalyptic statement by the apostle John is a Spirit-inspired exposition of the first promised deliverance from satanic power that Satan himself received in Genesis 3:15. The age-long struggle has been between the Seed of the woman and the seed of the serpent, and the ultimate victory belongs to the Seed of the woman.

Before examining areas of our lives in which Satan attacks us, we need to look first at Public Enemy Number One. Neither his methods and character nor the effectiveness of the weapons God has given us to use against him has changed since the beginning of time.

In Revelation 11, the more outward aspects of the great battle between the seed of the serpent and the seed of the woman are evident. There the conflict is visible. Now we are brought to the hidden, secret, spiritual, and even supernatural aspects of the struggle. The war no longer involves physical forms as in the struggle outlined in Revelation 12. The battle is against invisible forces and can be won only by the use of spiritual weapons.

We are not, of course, presently concerned about the prophetic application of this chapter. Revelation is a book of wars that can give us insights we can use in the war with our Enemy. Here we have what John Bunyan called "The Holy War." It is what Revelation 13 calls ". . . war with the saints . . ." (v. 7). Let us look at five aspects of this grim conflict.

THE SATANIC FOE

The character of the one in battle against us is clearly revealed in Revelation 12. The mask is torn from his ugly, hell-marked face. Our sinister spiritual foe has been sketched by a divine hand.

The great red dragon (Rev. 12:3)

The portrayal of this dreadful reptile with its seven heads, ten horns, and the seven crowns upon its head, suggests a fearsome and brutal force. The figure represents a dread and hostile power, one remorseless in the destruction of his foes.

He is depicted as a *red* dragon. Red is the color of flame and blood, the symbol of destruction and slaughter. Here is one, then, athirst for human blood, and truly Satan is athirst for blood. He is fierce, cruel, murderous. Jesus declared him to be a murderer from the beginning.

The seven heads, ten horns, and seven crowns imply that Satan is assisted by those sovereigns and powers animated by his spirit. World empires are under his control (see Eph. 6:10–12).

The old serpent (Rev. 12:9)

Here John labels Satan with the instrument he employed for man's overthrow. The serpent is the emblem of an evil principle (see Gen. 3:1). In the word *old* we have a reference to Satan's historical connection with the race. As the *serpent* he is crafty, subtle, deep, cunning.

The Devil (Rev. 12:9)

The word *devil* means to cast or throw down, and John reveals how Satan is able to throw down, and how, ultimately, he is cast down (Rev. 20:10).

Satan (Rev. 12:9)

This name means "adversary," and Satan is the adversary of the Father, the Son, the Holy Spirit—and of the blood-washed saints. He is the open and declared adversary of all that is holy, the public enemy number one of the Christian.

Deceiver (Rev. 12:9)

The Devil is the prime mover in all deception, chaos, perplexity, unrest, and war. He is at the back of all agitation, responsible for worldwide ruin.

Accuser (Rev. 12:10)

In this role Satan appears before God as the accuser and adversary of the redeemed. He is at his diabolical work "night and day." Continually he brings indictments and accusations against the saints. He is not concerned whether his accusations are true or false, as we can see in his accusations against Job (see Job 19:2) and Joshua (Zech. 3:1).

Though Satan hates the presence of God, he is willing to come before God to blacken our characters. We must be careful to give him no cause to accuse us. But if he has just cause, Christ is at the Father's right hand to plead His efficacious blood on our behalf (see 1 John 2:1; Rom. 8:33,34).

In Jewish writings Michael is called "The Advocate" who stands in opposition to "The Accuser." However, we have Jesus, an Advocate far mightier than a mere angel.

> *He signed the deeds with His atoning blood*
> *And ever lives to prove the judgment good;*
> *Should hell, or sin, or law come in*
> *   To argue second claim,*
> *They all withdraw at mention of His name.*

THE VALIANT WARRIORS

Who did John have in mind when he declared "they" overcame the enemy? It would seem as if he was referring to the "brethren" of verse 10. Prophetically, the promise covers those saints who will be on the earth during that period between the rapture of the church and the casting out of Satan.

But since Christ calls His people "brethren," such a term can include all those who have a blood relationship with the Lord. And since we are the Lord's brethren, we are objects of satanic hostility and can, if we will, appropriate our Lord's victory over the foe.

THE PERFECT DEFEAT

They *overcame* him! Do we believe in the defeatability of the Devil? Knowing that he is defeatable, do we successfully resist him? Archbishop Trevel reminds us that the image of the Christian as a conqueror, that is, as one who overcomes, is frequently in Paul's writings (see 1 Cor. 9:24,25; 2 Tim. 2:5). John, however, employs an exclusive word to express our moral victory over sin and all hellish forces.

The dictionary explains the word *overcome* as "to get the better of," "to conquer," "to subdue," "to be victorious." And it is Calvary that enables us to lord it over Satan. We march, not *on to* victory, as we sometimes sing, but *from* victory, for we are kept by the power of God.

THE VICTORIOUS WEAPONS

We have three weapons of our warfare, and such a threefold cord can never be broken or successfully resisted. Here, then, are the three marks of overcomers in all ages.

The blood is their *shelter*, giving them boldness before God (see Ex. 12:13).

The Word is their *weapon*, giving them boldness before Satan (see Eph. 6:17).

Love is their *power*, giving them boldness before men (see 2 Cor. 5:14).

But let us examine these victorious weapons more closely.

The blood of the Lamb

What do we mean by "the blood"? The communion service of the Church of England expresses it, "A full, perfect, and sufficient sacrifice, oblation, and satisfaction for the sins of the whole world which Christ, our Savior, made there upon the cross by His own oblation of Himself once offered."

By "the blood," then, we are to understand the work of Calvary in its fullness and finality. As the life is in the blood, so the cross represents the surrender of the perfect life of our sinless Lord, whereby man could be redeemed from the penalty, power, and presence of sin and forever rescued from the power of Satan.

When John writes that "they overcame him by the blood," the word *by* means "owing to." Dr. Weymouth translates it "gained victory because of" the blood. Thus we conquer on account of Calvary, whereby Christ destroyed death and the Devil.

There is a Jewish tradition that says Satan accuses men all days of the year except the "Day of Atonement," which was the day everything associated with the tabernacle was sprinkled with blood. Since we have a perpetual Day of Atonement, perpetual deliverance from the accusations of the Devil can be ours. The question is, are we living victorious lives because of the blood? We may proclaim belief in the doctrine of atonement and yet be destitute of the victory it supplies.

The word of their testimony

This weapon supplies boldness before Satan, as can be seen when Christ used it against His foe in the wilderness. The Word of God is the effectual sword of the Spirit. The infallible Scriptures and our testimony to them are invincible weapons. "They overcame him" by the Word to which they bore witness.

The powerful preaching of the Word and the living out of the Word are mighty instruments of war pulling down the strongholds of Satan. And this weapon is an outgrowth of the first weapon. Had there been no blood, there could have been no Book. When the Book is believed in, obeyed, and witnessed to, then we live in triumph. With a life exhibiting the truth, our enemies are forced to live in peace with us.

They did not love their lives to the death

Surely it is a mistake to identify overcomers as martyred saints only. John's description can represent all those who are devoted to the Master.

There is such a thing as living martyrdom, a daily losing of one's life for Christ's sake. Paul refers to those who are killed all the day long (see Rom. 8:36). Sudden death for the truth is preferable to the long drawn-out, agonizing martyrdom of saints like Pastor Niemoller, who languished in a German concentration camp.

Matthew Henry has this pithy comment:

> When love of life stood in competition with their loyalty to Christ, they loved not their lives so well but they could give them up to death, could lay them down, in Christ's cause. Their love of their own lives was overcome by stronger affections of another nature and so contributed to their victory.

They loved not themselves! Self-pleasure, self-inclinations, self-ease, self-will, self-interests, all wither

21

before Calvary. Dr. Weymouth translates the phrase, "They hold their lives cheap." Do we? Is everything subordinated to the Crucified? Do we coddle—or crucify—self? We must not only believe in a crucified Christ but also live a crucified life, if we would be more than conquerors.

THE TRIUMPHANT SONG

The defeat of Satan in the heavenly conflict draws out a burst of praise. Victorious saints celebrate their triumph over Satan with a glorious doxology. "Therefore rejoice, O heavens . . ." (v. 12).

Yes, and if we are jubilantly victorious, then we can expect the rage of Satan. What brings joy in the heavenlies brings woe to earth. Deliverance and delight go hand in hand. The saints can sing as they emerge victorious from a satanic struggle, ". . . I have redeemed thee, Sing, O ye heavens . . ." (Is. 44:22,23).

Christ Himself, anticipating the cross, with its mastery of hellish forces, went out to the bloody arena after singing a hymn (see Mark 14:26).

The same satanic foe described by John is battling believers today. But the same victory can be ours by using the same weapons of God's keeping power. Use them and sing a triumphant song of praise to the One who was a victor at Calvary.

Chapter 3

THE VISION SPLENDID

Paul wrote, ". . . I know whom I have believed and am persuaded that He is able to keep what I have committed to Him until that Day" (2 Tim. 1:12). We usually think of God's keeping power in terms of what God can do for us in specific areas of our lives. Indeed, we will be looking at how His power keeps us through worry, temptation, and other snares of the Devil. But we must realize that God's keeping power starts with a commitment by us as the result of a vision of God.

In Isaiah 6, the prophet recounts the circumstances by which he became a prophet of God and how his authority as a prophet was received. This chapter also indicates how every true servant of God is prepared by the Lord for the service to which he is called, whether it be as a missionary, preacher, teacher, Christian worker, or witness in a secular job or at home.

Within the chapter is one vision, yet there are three distinct aspects of it. Taken together these aspects declare the divine method of shaping lives. In verses 1–4 is the vision of a *throne;* in verses 5–7 is the vision of a *heart;* and in verses 8–13 is the vision of a *sphere.* In these three aspects of "The Vision Splendid" we come to know how saints are made and how servants are fashioned so that God might keep what they "have committed to Him until that Day."

THE VISION OF A THRONE

> In the year that king Uzziah died I saw also the Lord sitting upon a throne, high and lifted up, and his train filled the temple. Above it stood the seraphims: each one had six wings; with twain he covered his face, and with twain he covered his feet, and with twain he did fly. And one cried unto another, and said, Holy, holy, holy, is the LORD of hosts: the whole earth is full of his glory. And the posts of the door moved at the voice of him that cried, and the house was filled with smoke (Is. 6:1–4).

It is essential for us to begin here. We must have our vision transferred from an earthly throne to the heavenly throne. Our eyes must be taken away from things earthly and focused upon God Himself. If our life is not saintly, it is because we do not have a vision of the Lord in all His glorious fullness. We only triumph in life when we can sing, "My goal is God Himself; not peace, nor joy, nor blessing, but Himself—my God!"

A defective vision of the Lord always means a defective saintliness in life. Our knowledge and vision of God determine the quality of our life.

I would remind you of two things regarding the vision of a throne. The first is that vacancy results in vision. "In the year that king Uzziah died I saw also the Lord. . . ." A crisis brought the prophet to the realization that God is supreme. With the death of the earthly king, Isaiah came to know something of the holiness, power, and sovereignty of the heavenly King. The visible monarch had to be made invisible before the invisible Monarch was made visible to the prophet. Paradoxically, Isaiah saw the Lord high and lifted up not through the open window of heaven, but down through an open grave.

We frequently talk about being "up and doing," but that is not the language of the Scriptures. The only way by which we can know what it is to be exalted by the Lord Himself is to be "down and dying." Through the grave we catch a glorious glimpse of the Lord as the abiding Friend. If it is not the grave of a dear one, then it is a grave in which we bury our hopes and ambitions—a grave in which we are willing to bury self. We cannot expect that God will give us a vision until we are willing to vacate from our lives those earthly things on which we depend.

A friend came to George Müller and asked him the secret of his power and fruitfulness. That mighty man of prayer replied, "There came a day when I was brought to realize that George Müller must die." Out of his own grave, he received a vision of the all-sufficiency of God.

Vacancy, then, brings vision. Tears become our telescope, and through them we have a clearer vision of the majesty of the Lord. The tomb leads to a throne. God often empties the earthly sphere that He may fill it with more of His own glorious, abiding presence. We must learn to let every vacancy in life bring to us the all-inclusive vision of the glory of God.

Second, I would remind you of the vastness of the vision granted to the prophet. What a glorious description we have in this chapter of the Lord, high and lifted up! In fact, it was the Lord Jesus Christ Himself whom the prophet saw, for in John 12:41 the apostle tells us that Isaiah saw the glory of Jesus and spoke of Him.

See how He is depicted here: In verse 1 the Lord is sitting upon a throne "and his train filled the temple." In verse 3 He is revealed as the thrice Holy One. In verse 5 Isaiah is given a glimpse of His power: ". . . mine eyes have seen the King, the LORD of hosts." In verse 7 we are brought face to face with His loving-kindness and tender mercies, for He was willing to forgive the iniquity of His servant. And verse 8 indicates the blessed truth of the Trinity: "Whom shall I send, and who will go for *us*?" And from verse 9 to the end of the chapter, God is seen as the God of judgment.

Doubtless you have noticed while studying Isaiah 6, that when the prophet speaks of the earthly king the translators use a small "k": "In the year that king Uzziah died. . . ." But in verse 5, when Isaiah refers to the heavenly King, the translators use a capital "K": ". . . mine eyes have seen the King, the LORD of hosts." And that is as it should be. For the best of earth pales into insignificance before the splendor of the King of kings and Lord of lords.

"Mine eyes have seen the King." Do you have a "King" in your life with a capital "K"? Do you know the Lord Jesus as the Sovereign of every part of your life? You may know Him as Savior and yet not recognize Him as the Sovereign of your life. Have you given Jesus His coronation? Have you crowned Him Lord of all? "If He is not Lord *of* all, then He is not Lord *at* all," someone has rightly said. Have your eyes seen Him as a King? Does He reign without a rival over your empire of love? If you know Him as your King, the One who is majestic, holy, powerful, loving, all-glorious, and high

26

above all forces, then the vacancies of earth will not cause you unnecessary trouble and sorrow, disappointment and despair.

Isaiah's difficulty was that he had lost a friend. He had learned to depend upon king Uzziah. He had often counselled with him. How could he face the future without him? What was he to do now that the king was dead? Only by means of the grave were his eyes opened to see the all-glorious King above.

Often this is our difficulty. "What am I going to do if my husband is taken from me or if some dear one is removed?" What are you to do in such a vacancy? Look to the Lord, for amid all the separations that may come to us He will remain. "What am I going to do if I lose my work and circumstances go against me?" What are you to do? See also the Lord.

When the news announcing the death of D. L. Moody reached the Bible Institute which today bears his name, Dr. Torrey went into the office of Mr. Gaylord, the business manager, and said, "Gaylord, Mr. Moody is dead. What are we going to do?" He was thinking of the heavy responsibility of carrying on the work that God had blessed through the labors of D. L. Moody. The two men dropped to their knees and committed the entire responsibility to God. Although D. L. Moody died, there came to those two men a vision of all that the Lord was willing to do in the work He had made possible.

Often we speak that way: "Our minister seems to be indispensable. He is a marvelous pastor, and we love his preaching. We do not know what the church is going to do if the Lord removes him." Never forget that although God removes His workmen, He always carries on His work. When God takes a Moses to be with Him, there is always a Joshua ready to fill his place. God does not die when friends leave us. Amid all vacancies, He remains. The empty throne caused the prophet Isaiah to have a vision of the Lord: ". . . mine eyes have seen the King, the LORD of hosts." Have you seen Him as the Lord of hosts? He is supreme over all heavenly forces, over all hellish forces, and over all human forces.

The prophet saw Christ *sitting* upon a throne, indicating His victory and supremacy. "The Lord God Omnipotent reigns." Let the earth tremble.

THE VISION OF A HEART

Then said I, Woe is me! for I am undone; because I am a man of unclean lips, and I dwell in the midst of a people of unclean lips: for mine eyes have seen the King, the LORD of hosts. Then flew one of the seraphims unto me, having a live coal in his hand, which he had taken with the tongs from off the altar: And he laid it upon my mouth, and said, Lo, this hath touched thy lips; and thine iniquity is taken away, and thy sin purged (Is. 6:5–8).

As the prophet Isaiah looked down into the open grave of Uzziah, his eyes were directed up to the Lord. After gazing at the exalted throne, he could look down into the depths of his own being. His eyes were directed from that empty earthly throne to the filled heavenly throne, and then to the throne of his own heart.

What great verses these are! They are to be read and studied when we are upon our knees, alone with the King Himself. Do you have the viewpoint of heaven concerning your own life? Isaiah could see the throne of his heart in the light of the throne above. Do we guide and shape our lives by human standards? Or do we look at the throne within our hearts in the light radiating from the throne occupied by the King of kings?

First, Isaiah's vision of the Lord resulted in an understanding of the prophet's own vileness. ". . . Woe is me! for I am undone . . . mine eyes have seen the King, the LORD of hosts." The vision of the heavenly King caused Isaiah to see his own heart. Sunlight reveals the dirt in a room as it never could be seen if the blinds were drawn. In the same way, the majesty and holiness of the Lord, whose train filled the temple, revealed the loathsome uncleanness of the prophet. Through the vision of the love of the Lord, the prophet came to understand something of the unloveliness of his own heart.

So it has always been with the saints of God. Seeing the Lord as He is, they have seen themselves as they are. God caused His glory and majesty to pass before Job with the result that the patriarch cried, "I abhor myself" (Job 42:6). Peter one day had a manifestation of the power of his Master, and it led him to cry, "Depart from me, for I am a sinful man, O Lord!" (Luke 5:8). The apostle John had a vision of the Savior in all His majesty, and the apostle says, "When I saw Him, I fell at His feet as dead . . ." (Rev. 1:17). The vision of the Lord always results in a vision of our own loathsomeness. "Woe is me! for I am undone; because I am a man of unclean lips."

Do you know what it is to understand your own evil heart as the result of seeing the holiness of the Lord? The Scottish poet craved for power to see himself as others saw him, but that is not the divine method. We must see ourselves as God sees us! And we can never accomplish very much in life for God unless we have a vision of our own condition and need.

Isaiah's vision of the Lord also revealed the weakest spot in his life. Notice how personal the prophet is in this confession. "Woe is me! for I am undone; because I am a man of unclean lips. . . ." The sin that the prophet was made conscious of, as the result of his vision, was the sin of his lips. It is my firm conviction that lip-sin is the greatest of all sins in the pathway of the saints. James makes this very clear in that remarkable epistle of his.

Isaiah does not say how he had sinned with his lips. Perhaps he had murmured and complained against God about the removal of king Uzziah, for he had been very friendly with the king. It may be that, like Moses, he spoke unwisely. The tragedy with some people is that their lips continue to speak and sing, although their lives are not clean and consistent. But if lip-sin had been a conspicuous sin of the prophet, the vision seemed to have silenced him, for, as Bishop Lowth translates that verse, Isaiah said, "I am silenced." And so for the time being, his lips were closed.

Third, Isaiah's vision of the Lord opened his eyes to the nature of his environment. ". . . I am a man of unclean lips, and I dwell in the midst of a people of unclean lips. . . ." Mark the order! Isaiah saw the throne of the Lord most high. Then he looked down into his own heart, and seeing the need of his own heart, he looked out and viewed those around him as God saw them. He saw that humanity was a reflection of his own nature. If you look long enough you will discover that the corruption around you is but a reflection of your own heart.

The only way by which we can discover the need of others is to see the Lord in His august holiness, and in the light of His holiness understand the deep need of our own hearts. The more I understand this old Adamic nature of mine in the light streaming from the throne, the more sympathetic I become toward the sins and the failures of those around me. Nothing can make us more sympathetic with the shortcomings of others than a more thorough knowledge of our own hearts and lives. There are social reformers who try to see the need of those around them, but they are blind to the world of iniquity within their own hearts.

Finally, Isaiah's vision of the Lord resulted in his cleansing. The seraphim came with a live coal from the altar and placed it upon the lips of the prophet. By this Isaiah was made conscious of the fact that he needed cleansing. Then he heard the voice of the seraphim, ". . . this hath touched thy lips; and thine iniquity is taken away, and thy sin purged."

Vision, then vileness, then victory. That is always the divine order. Here is an example of the full deliverance of the sinning saint who desires to be fully cleansed and equipped for service.

Be sure to notice two things in this chapter: a throne in verse 1 and an altar in verse 6. You can never have a throne-life unless you know something of the altar-life. You can never share the throne life of God unless you know something of the altar of God. The altar speaks about the sacrifice of Christ and the way by which cleansing can reach us. The live coal represents the mighty ministry of the Holy Spirit, for He it is who applies the gracious work of cleansing to the soul of the believer who desires to be sanctified.

A devoted missionary said to an educated Chinese, "Do you mind telling me what China's greatest need is?" After a moment's reflection the Chinese gentleman said, "Yes, China's greatest need is a company of men

and women with hot hearts to tell the story of Jesus."
The world today needs believers who have seen a vision
of the Lord, seen their own vileness and the evil in the
world around them, and have won victory by the sanc-
tifying work of the Holy Spirit.

THE VISION OF A SPHERE

"Also I heard the voice of the Lord, saying, Whom
shall I send, and who will go for us? Then said I, Here
am I; send me" (Is. 6:8).

We tend to reverse the divine method. We want a
sphere of service before we discover our sin and experience the cleansing of the Lord. We want to say to the
Lord, "Here am I; send me," before we cry, "Woe is
me." But "woe is me" precedes "send me." You can
never have a vocation until you know something about
the vision. This is the divine order:

> *Vision*—"I saw the Lord."
> *Vileness*—"I am a man of unclean lips."
> *Victory*—"Thy sin is purged."
> *Vocation*—"Here am I; send me."

God will never plunge you into the depths of human
need until you have entered into the depths of your
own need and discovered the fullness of God. Washing
is before witness. Cleansing is before commission.
Purging is before proclamation. There is no need to fear
that God will not have the right kind of workers, or that
those workers are not in the right sphere, if first of all
there has been the vision of a throne and the vision of a
heart.

Let us first of all note that the service of a cleansed, surrendered saint is always voluntary. God did not command Isaiah to go; He asked, "Whom shall I send, and who will go for us?" Remember that we labor in partnership with the Trinity. With the call there came the response, for immediately Isaiah replied, "Here am I; send *me.*" Or, as the original has it, "Behold me; send me."

Never forget, there are no drafted men or women in the service of God; they are all volunteers. All who serve the Lord with untiring devotion are those captivated by the vision splendid and are always ready to offer lips and lives in obedience to the divine call.

Some people translate this verse, "Here am I, Lord. Send somebody else." There is a great lack of willing service. I have no sympathy with those Christians who have to be urged and coddled into service, who shrink from their own personal responsibility, who are not willing to serve the Lord with eagerness. Such willingness is the evidence of a deficient vision. The service of one fully surrendered is always voluntary and enthusiastic.

Second, we should note that when we volunteer, the Lord may not always assign us to agreeable service. Think of what Isaiah had to do. He had the vision of a throne, then the vision of his own heart, and then there came the readiness and willingness to serve the Lord. God did not tell him to gather in multitudes, but to

... Go, and tell this people, Hear ye indeed, but understand not; and see ye indeed, but perceive not. Make the heart of this people fat, and make their ears heavy, and shut their eyes; lest they see with their eyes, and hear with their ears, and understand with their heart, and convert, and be healed (vv. 9,10).

So the prophet's new commission, received as the result of his vision, was very undesirable and unauspicious and unresponsive. God's hard places are difficult to fill. That's why God calls for volunteers. The person who has seen the King and whose life is completely surrendered is willing to follow the Lord wherever He may direct. Some people like to have the best places, the easiest spheres, but the obedient servant goes whether the sphere is pleasant or unpleasant, lucrative or otherwise. To see the King means to go anywhere, as long as we know we are accomplishing a divinely-appointed task.

You may be preparing for Christian service. But when your training is over, God may call you to a very unpleasant sphere of labor in some very uncomfortable surroundings, just as He called the prophet Isaiah. He may ask you to serve Him with little visible result. According to tradition, Isaiah declared the Word of God in such a sphere and later was sawn in two by his own son-in-law, Manasseh.

I think of John and Betty Stam of China. During their training at the Moody Bible Institute they had a vision of the Lord; they saw something of His majesty and greatness coming down from the throne above to the throne of their own hearts, and they knew what it was to crown the Lord Jesus as King of their lives. The day came when they responded to His call, "Whom shall I send to China?" and they said, "Here are we, Lord; send us." And He sent them! What for? To live for a few months in that needy land of China and then to depart to be with Christ in glory. The hands of the cruel men who brutally killed their bodies were not able to kill their souls. The Stams were willing to lay down their lives for His name's sake.

God may lay hold of you and bury you in the heart of some city slum, there to work day after day with little visible result. Or He may ask you to live amid the antagonism of your home where you find no sympathy. Are you ready? Have your eyes seen the King? Have you discovered your own inward need? Have you the knowledge of the cleansing blood and the purging fire upon your lips and life? Then, and only then, are you ready to respond, "Here am I, Lord; send me." And wherever He sends you, whatever He asks you to do, you can know with assurance that He will keep what you have committed until the day of His glorious appearing.

The vision of a throne, the vision of a heart, the vision of a sphere! May you know what it is to be borne along by the vision splendid and the keeping power of God.

Chapter 4

DYING TO LIVE

Years ago I came across a sign that impressed me outside a dyers and bleachers establishment:

We live to dye
We dye to live.

It reminded me of Paul's great declaration, "For if you *live* according to the flesh, you will *die*; but if you through the Spirit put to death the deeds of the body, you will *live*" (Rom. 8:13, italics added).

The saint must not live to die, that is, live after the flesh and die spiritually. Rather he must "die to live," that is, die to the flesh that he might live spiritually.

Victory over sin and self is one of the dominating themes of the Bible, explained in various ways by teachers of "holiness." The truest definition of sanctification, however, is the one Paul was fond of using, namely, as a double process of dying and living. Ours must be a life in which the old nature is daily subdued, put to death, and the new nature daily strengthened, perfected, made to live. Christ must increase, self decrease.

In considering the sacred theme before us, we need to preserve balance, and not emphasize one phase at the expense of another. There is a tendency in some quarters to dwell on the death side and to neglect the resurrection side. But we must understand both sides of this means to victory and hold fast to both in knowledge and experience.

Although it is by God's power that we are kept until His glorious appearing, nevertheless He expects us to submit our will to His. It is essential, therefore, that we understand the twofold process of victory over sin and the ways God has given us of appropriating this victory.

THE TWOFOLD PROCESS

Dying, we live! Living, we die! If we put to death the deeds of the flesh, we will live. All injunctions and commands to holy living talk about either putting to death our flesh or becoming alive by being more like Christ. Let us consider some passages where the death and life sides of victory are set forth.

Bishop Moule translates Romans 8:13: "If ye are living flesh-wise you are on the way to die. But if by the Spirit you are putting to death the practices, the stratagems, the machinations of the body, you will live."

The body of the believer is still the seat and vehicle of temptation and of sin. The believer never has a day when he is free from evil, residing not merely around but within him. But by habitually remembering and appropriating the Holy Spirit, he is able to put to death the practices of the flesh.

The phrase "put to death" is in the present tense, implying that the process is a continuing one—one that will go on until we leave this earth. The ideal life, then, is one in which we have a daily death and a daily resurrection. We live and die daily.

Another significant passage is Romans 12:2, in which we are urged not to ". . . be conformed to this world but be transformed by the renewing of your mind. . . ." We are not to become like the worldly people around us in the way we think and act—this is the death side of victory. Christ died for us, saved us, not to reconcile us to the world, but to make us opposite of the world, dissimilar, estranged to it at every point.

". . . Be transformed by the renewing of your mind. . . ." This phrase implies that we are to live a life as distinct from our old life in the world as physical life is distinct from physical death. And, here again, we have the idea of a continuous process, seeing that the words used are in the present tense. The life of the saint is one of constant progressive death to the world and daily transformation into Christlikeness.

In his Colossian letter, Paul approached from another angle this dual process by which we have victory over sin: ". . . raised with Christ, [we must] seek those things which are above. . . . you died. . . . Therefore put to death your members which are on the earth" (Col. 3:1,3,5). Here, two practical conclusions are emphasized: The death Christ died must be made real in ourselves, and His resurrection must become a mighty factor in our daily lives. This twofold truth can be illustrated from nature. Scientists tell us, for instance, that death is constantly going on within the human body. We change cells every seven years. Every day a certain amount of living tissue dies and has to be borne out to burial, and every day new tissue is formed.

Death and life are likewise the universal law of nature. Seeds die that fragrant flowers and luscious fruit may appear. Animals die that men may live. Our Lord Himself used nature to illustrate the death and life process: ". . . unless a grain of wheat falls into the ground and dies, it remains alone; but if it dies, it produces much grain" (John 12:24).

> *Life evermore is fed by death*
> *In earth and sea and sky,*
> *And, that a rose may breathe its breath*
> *Something must die.*

The concepts of "death" and "life" form the foundation of our Christian faith and life. The apostle Paul sets forth the gospel he was commissioned to preach in these two focal facts, ". . . Christ died for our sins. . . . He rose again the third day . . ." (1 Cor. 15:3,4). And the historic facts must become spiritual realities if we are to become victorious Christians. Christ died that we might die to the practices of the flesh and to the appeal of sin. He died *for* sin that we might die *to* sin. He died *for* the world that we might be dead *to* the world (see Gal. 6:4).

In one sense crucifixion was not finished at Calvary. The death of the cross will continue until the church is completely saved and sins no more. The cross must be taken up daily. Likewise, the resurrection is also prolonged. "The church," says a devout writer, "keeps perpetual Easter." Every soul born again is a pulsebeat of the crucified, risen Lord on the throne. But can we truly sing: "Dying with Jesus by death reckoned mine,/ Living with Jesus a new life divine"?

As an Irishman passed a graveyard he remarked to his friend, "Sure, and that's the place where the dead live." And Romans 6,7,8 are the chapters where the dead must live. Constant identification with Christ in His death and resurrection is the place where all who would die to sin and self must live. Of course, we should remember that sin and self do not die, but by the Spirit we die to them.

THE FIVEFOLD SECRET

It is encouraging to know that we are not left to mere discipline or to the exercise of our own willpower to bring to the place of death the deeds of the body. Moving from death to life does not come by our own efforts. The life of the believer presents a battlefield. But rather than a struggle to victory, it is a continuous march to victory. What are the secrets of this victorious attitude?

1. *Meditating upon Christ*

Beholding the glory of the Lord, says Paul, we are being transformed (see 2 Cor. 3:18). While it is true that a glance at our Lord is enough to save a person, as the testimony of the dying thief at Calvary proves, it takes a prolonged gaze at Christ to produce sanctification.

Augustine, commenting upon God's statement to Moses, ". . . for there shall no man see me, and live" (Ex. 33:20), remarks, "Then let me die if only I may see His face." We appropriate God's power over sin by gazing at Christ and dying to sin and self. Seeing Him, we fall at His feet as dead.

We are able to discern the glory of His holy countenance to the degree to which we put to death the deeds of the flesh. "Blessed are the pure in heart,/For they shall see God" (Matt. 5:8). Clarity of vision depends upon purity of heart. Long association with a friend produces a likeness to that friend. Thus it is in the spiritual realm. The more we contemplate Christ, the greater our likeness will be to Him.

Alas, however, people of this age suffer from bloodshot, world-blinded eyes. We have lost the most difficult of all arts, namely, meditation upon abiding things. It is only as we turn our eyes upon Jesus that the things of earth grow strangely dim.

2. *The appropriation of Christ*

A mystic truth, so hard for the carnal mind to appreciate, is the one our Lord uttered, "He who feeds on Me will live because of me." The story is told of a sick soldier who had given up to die. His father hurried from a long distance to his son's bedside where he lay, barely conscious. Nothing the father or attendants said aroused the lad until the father happened to say, "Here is a loaf of your mother's bread which I have brought you." "Bread from home," cried the dying son, "give me some!" And from that time he began to mend.

Our Bread from heaven is the crucified, risen, glorified Christ. If we would live, we must feed upon the promises of the gospel, the Christ of the gospel, and the hope of the gospel. In order to die to all that is alien to God's holy will, and live as unto Him, we must daily feed on Him who is our Bread.

3. *Abiding in Christ*

In the parable of the vine, two aspects of our life in Christ are distinguishable. There is *union*, "abide in

42

Me," and *communion*, "I in you" (John 15:4). Our position and practice are both emphasized.

It is utterly impossible to make death to sin a reality by a mere imitation of Christ. There must come an incorporation into Christ; we become part of Him and His Spirit lives in us just as a branch is part of a vine. One may sit down before the most perfect portrait of Jesus ever painted and sing, "Let the beauty of Jesus be seen in me," but nothing will happen. Likeness to Christ comes from the Holy Spirit and by unbroken union and communion with our beautiful Lord Himself.

We readily admit that there are a good many moral, religious people who are like Christ in their actions, but such actions are simply the product of the natural man. Holiness, however, can never be produced by human effort: It is a gift of God. The greatest enemy of holiness is morality. One can be moral without being holy, but never holy without being moral. We die to the old habits, old natural interests, to our good and bad self, only as life flows into us from the Vine.

4. *The coming of Christ*

The apostle John reminds us that another method of victory over sin is our acceptance of the truth of our Lord's return. If we have such a hope within our hearts, then we become pure, even as Christ Himself is pure (see 1 John 3:1–3).

Our daily purity corresponds to our daily expectancy of the Master's return. The Second Advent exercises a powerful influence over our life. It is effective in making us dead to worldly, sinful pursuits and practices. With such a blessed hope in view, we become more holy in life. The anticipation of Christ's appearing lifts us out of all that is low, selfish, and unholy, and into activities and motives that are serene, blessed, and God-glorifying. A blessed, victorious life is inspired by the nearness of Christ's return.

5. *The Spirit of Christ*

Dying to sin and self and becoming alive to a likeness of Christ are not possible without the gracious aid of the Holy Spirit, Lord and Life-Giver. The indwelling Spirit possessing the believer is a divine, all-effectual counter-agent to all the encumbering influences of the flesh. Victory and holiness are always "by the Spirit" (see Rom. 8:13; 2 Cor. 3:18).

As the Spirit fills the life, the habits of the self-life disappear. "The law of the Spirit of life in Christ Jesus has made me free from the law of sin and death" (Rom. 8:2).

God's power for victory over sin comes from dying and living. Can we say that we are dying to live? Is the old life growing less through the mortification of the flesh? Is the new life daily increasing through the constant appropriation of the glorified Christ? Are we being made conformable to His death? Do we share the power of His resurrection? "I live, yet not I!" May the constant realization of this dual truth be ours!

Chapter 5

MEETING AND MASTERING TEMPTATION

Temptation proves the existence of a tempter, whom Scriptures tell us is Satan. With a diabolical hatred, the enemy strives to erase the multitudes of earth by subtle methods and temptations. God loves to bless; Satan is out to blast.

Temptation is a constant battle in our warfare with the enemy. It is never over while we are on this earth. Yet here too God's keeping power can give us victory.

A UNIVERSAL EXPERIENCE

There are six aspects of temptation to which we must draw our attention. The first is, *we will be tempted*. One of the first experiences we meet in the Bible, and in life, is temptation. All are tempted. Some may be more immune than others. In such people there appears to be the enjoyment of comparative calm, yet the biblical declaration remains true—temptation is common to man.

Temptations conform to one's temperament. What attracts one person would never seduce another. Temptations likewise vary according to age. Some temptations are outlived. What tempted us when we were young has no influence over us in old age. And then, environment plays an important part in the form of temptation aimed at us. Solitude has its temptations as does society. A preacher's library can be as dangerous as the marketplace. Satan is a master at his work. He knows how to vary his approach and adapt his plans to each person. Every person's well-being depends upon the attitude he assumes toward temptation.

The second aspect is, *all of us have fallen before temptation.* Temptation, like sorrow, pain, and death, is a common experience. Our own hearts are witness to the fact that at some time or other we have all yielded to the enemy. Our willpower and self-resistance were insufficient. We sadly confess that we could no more empty our hearts of evil than bale darkness out of a room.

Then, we have to admit that *we have been guilty of tempting others.* Influence, we have learned, can never be neutral. Defeated ourselves, weaker souls have suffered as a result of our fall.

Moreover, as we are to see more fully, *temptation can be successfully resisted.* Our temptations can be turned into stepping stones leading to nobility of character. By divine grace, all of us can be victors in the hour of conflict.

It may be possible to move away, by our own power, from some phases of temptation. But as one old Puritan divine said, "The greatest of all temptations is to be without any."

Last of all, *our victory greatly assists others who are struggling to overcome their temptations.* Inspired by our God-given deliverance, the defeated souls around us take courage.

THE NATURE OF TEMPTATION

If the stainless heart of Jesus was not immune from the assault of the cunning and crafty foe, then because my nature is human and my world is what it is, Satan is bound to haunt and dog my steps. But what, exactly, is temptation? To express it simply, temptation is sin presented. Sin is temptation yielded to. Temptation, then, is not sin. We cannot sin without being tempted. We can, however, be tempted and yet not sin. That Sunday school hymn we used to sing crystallizes the truth:

> *Yield not to temptation*
> *For yielding is sin,*
> *Each victory will help you*
> *Some other to win.*

Temptation is the factory where God fashions His saints. Of course, God does not send temptation. But He wisely permits it that we may become holier and more useful to Him. Here is truly a beautiful picture of the way in which we can let God turn evil desires into events that glorify Himself. Through temptation, the Devil would drag us down to hell. Yet, by it, God seeks to draw us nearer heaven.

THE METHOD OF TEMPTATION

Temptation, as we have indicated, is either a sharp tool of destruction or a polished shaft. First of all, temptation works *in* us. It either makes or mars, develops or degrades our character. It can become a door to saintliness or ungodliness, as we decide. Our first parents

47

yielded to temptation and thereby brought sorrow and death into the world. Joseph was sorely tempted, but by scorning Potiphar's wife who tried to seduce him he ennobled his character to the glory of God.

Temptation is splendid discipline if met and overcome by the Holy Spirit. But without heavenly aid to resist, temptation becomes our master; yielding to it changes good into evil and light into darkness. The Lord permits but never sends temptation. And with His permission there is always provisional grace to overcome.

Temptation also works *through* us to tempt others. The Devil's means of temptation is through the lives and influence of those who have already fallen. Not satisfied with his own fall, Satan brings about the fall of others, angels and men.

If we have yielded to temptation ourselves, we invariably try to drag others down. Sin hates solitude. There are some who curse the hour they met certain people, for it was through them they saw and ate the forbidden fruit. Jesus reserves especially harsh words for those through whom temptation works: "Whoever causes one of these little ones who believe in Me to sin, it would be better for him if a millstone were hung around his neck, and he were drowned in the depth of the sea" (Matt. 18:6).

Sometimes the one we admire best and love the most becomes unconsciously the tool of Satan. The enemy came directly to Job without success. Yet through his wife Job was tempted to curse God and die. Jesus had to say to Peter, "Get behind Me, Satan." Behind Peter's innocent suggestion, Jesus detected the wiles of Satan.

Is it not a solemn thought that our life directs others either to Christ or to Satan? No man lives unto himself.

Our influence is never neutral. Our witness is a signpost pointing heavenward or hellward. The greatest cause of fear among those passing into perdition will be that they are not in outer darkness alone. Others will be there to taunt them with the fact that it was their influence that brought them to desolation. What a terrible thing it will be to hear a voice saying, "I am damned, and I have you to thank for it."

On the other hand, one cause for joy in heaven will be the assurance that souls are there because of our consecrated witness. Through a sermon preached, a letter written, a word of encouragement spoken, or as the result of a silent, fragrant witness on earth, many will arise to call us blessed. "What is our . . . crown of rejoicing? Is it not even you in the presence of our Lord Jesus Christ at His coming?" (1 Thess. 2:19). It is for this we are kept by the power of God.

VICTORY OVER TEMPTATION

If we would emerge victoriously from a conflict with the enemy, we must know our weapons and how to use them. In His mercy, God has provided us with effective ways of escape. Praise His name, we are not left defenseless!

Watchfulness, for example, is essential to victory. "'Watch . . . lest you enter into temptation . . .'" (Matt. 26:41). We often fail because we do not watch for the beginnings of evil. One writer said, "Our greatest security against sin lies in being shocked at it." Much of our temptation comes subtly so that it is upon us before we are aware we are being tempted. Surprise attack is one of the principle methods the tempter employs, and because we are so often not on guard, he breaks through. How we need to have our eyes constantly anointed in order to detect his faintest approach!

Prayerfulness is also a safeguard. Satan trembles when he sees the saint upon his knees. A praying believer is a great hindrance to the Devil and his works. If we are constantly praying that temptation may not overwhelm us, it will be difficult for Satan to take us unaware.

Resistance is another avenue of victory. James reminds us that if we truly resist the Devil, he will flee from us. We must resist him, "at the very gate, on his first knocking." But how can we successfully resist our subtle foe? One effective method is simply to remember those who love us and pray for us. Thoughts of home and God have caused many to cry when tempted, "How can I be guilty of this wickedness and sin against God?" The story is told of a transformed criminal who always carried in his pocket the photograph of the godly lady who led him to Christ. When faced with temptation he would draw out the picture and say to himself, "No, I cannot do it. She would be grieved." How much more of an incentive to holy living should be our memory of Christ's love for us.

Then there is *conscience*, which, when under divine control, is a strong force to keep us from temptation. Conscience enabled Joseph to refuse the advances of Potiphar's wife. We look with admiration upon those who are heroes of war. And yet moral courage is greater than mere physical valor. Each of us has exhausting struggles that are secretly fought and won. Our neighbors may never learn of our secret conflicts, yet in God's eyes they shine more glorious than those of any battlefield. The world has no knowledge of our battles and victories. God, however, chronicles them in His book of honors.

Counter-attraction is another way of victory. If our hearts are constantly drawn to God and His Word, Satan's temptings will not hold as much interest for us. David sought to hide God's Word in his heart that he might not sin against the Lord. A mind steeped in God's Word and a life filled with God's Spirit are effective weapons against temptation, as our Lord's experience in the wilderness clearly proves.

Last of all, there is the *blood of the Lamb,* the mightiest weapon we have to wield against our arch-enemy as he seeks our overthrow. It is through the death of Christ on the cross that we have forgiveness of sins and the power to withstand temptation.

There is an old American Indian belief that whenever a warrior scalped an enemy the strength of the victim passed into the arm of the victor. Surely there is a parable here that we can apply to the moral conflict. "Each victory will help you, some other to win."

Are you being tempted right now? Then use the weapons God has given you for battle against the tempter and claim the victory Christ gave you at the cross. Be careful, however, to watch the tactics of Satan. Before we fall, he whispers that one slip will not matter. To taste forbidden fruit just once is a mere trifle. But this is tragic reasoning, for once we fall, something is lost we can never regain. Then, after we have fallen, Satan whispers that we may as well go the whole road. By creating despair, he tells us that it is hopeless trying to resist. But we should resist, for by the blood of the Lamb we can become more than conquerers. As we hurl his lie back at his face, we tell such a false accuser that

defeat can be transformed into a glorious victory, that
his fierce temptations can be made stepping stones to a
higher, nobler life. Robert Browning asks:

*Why comes temptation, but for man to meet
And master, and make crouch beneath his feet,
And so be pedestalled in triumph.*

Chapter 6

ON THE MONOTONY OF DAILY LIFE

David's career was certainly not a monotonous one. He was a king, a psalmist, a warrior, a musician, and a man after God's own heart. How many different changes were crowded into one life! No wonder he could write, "Because they do not change, / Therefore they do not fear God" (Ps. 55:19).

Most of us long for a life free from unpleasant change. We feel that a regular routine and a life of predictable sameness will bring us comfort so that we will be able to draw closer to God. We think that any person without change must be especially fortunate for "change and decay in all around we see." The world is the scene of perpetual change. The sun rises and sets; the moon waxes and wanes; the tides rise and fall; seedtime and harvest, summer and winter, day and night all come and go.

Change comes to all of us, and so we cannot take the psalmist's words in a strictly literal sense. Yet there are those who experience less change than others. The changes of which David speaks are those changes we least expect or desire: changes that disturb, unhinge our plans and arrangements, and frustrate our hopes, changes which, like earthquakes, upheave all order, comfort, and settled ease.

But without such changes we are liable to drift into the perils of an undisturbed life. Pleasant monotony breeds ignorance of God. When a man's life is filled with blessings and is never darkened by storms and rent by numerous tumultuous sorrows, there is a danger that monotony will rob him of deeper holiness of life. When unexpected and disturbing change enters our lives, we are unlikely to recognize it as being part of God's plan to strengthen our exercise of His keeping power. Unexpected and unpleasant change is an opportunity for growth given by God. We must make the most of it.

THE VARIED CHANGES OF LIFE

David, as we have already said, was a man of many changes. Time and time again he was tried, and yet God favored him. Psalm 55, for instance, refers to the tragic era in the psalmist's life when he was betrayed by his trusted counsellors and his confidence was nearly shaken. But his trials drove him nearer to God. He knew only too well that uninterrupted prosperity, consistently good bodily health, and social success were apt to cause the neglect of higher things.

Worldly prosperity

We know there are those who devise plans and always succeed. All the vessels they launch have prosperous voyages and return heavily laden with rich cargo. They are like the legendary King Midas who turned everything he touched into gold. And, in some cases, these men of affluence are not very religious. Worldly in life, and not too particular about morality and honesty, they succeed where godly men fail.

We long for the monotony of continued prosperity, yet such prosperity often produces self-confidence and forgetfulness of God. When a person's heart has all it wishes for and freedom from impoverishing changes, the need of God is not perceived to be very acute. Unbroken prosperity is spiritually dangerous. A man who does nothing but win, prosper, get on, is seldom a chastened, spiritually refined, sympathetic soul. Uninterrupted, monotonous success breeds atheism. No changes mean no prayers! If one climbs the ladder of fame and riches, rung by rung, with no interruption caused by failure, the tendency is to boast in one's own wisdom and strength for that success. Then God is not feared and recognized as the Giver of all.

The paradox of faith, however, is that we are built by being broken down. God does by undoing. He makes as He breaks. Financial reverses and changes are tools God uses for shaping our character. God sometimes takes us back to move us forward.

Bodily health

There are those persons whose wealth is found in their health. A body free from sickness or pain is by far greater riches than silver. Such a treasure can become just as much a peril to one's spiritual life as material wealth. Perfectly healthy people are apt to forget that they are only a house of clay, and so they quickly expend their energy. The march of life is taken with the step and eye of a giant. Weariness, pain, and despondency never impede their progress. They boast, "I have never had a day's illness."

The world's spiritual giants, however, are not those who have never known a day's sickness, but they are the valiant army of courageous souls with broken health. A person with a healthy body seems to be more able to find plausible excuses for not lifting a sin-cursed world nearer to God.

Moreover, those who experience the monotony of always being healthy are often indifferent to the evident need of those who are suffering. Sometimes a strong man who has never had a day's sickness is not as considerate as he should be of a frail, sickly wife. Those who are healthy will find it more difficult to show compassion or understand pain. The people who best show sympathy are those who themselves suffer, whose bodies bear the marks of a surgeon's knife. The monotony of constant physical health makes it difficult to fear God and show compassion.

Social life

There are others who seem to have a circle of social life wonderfully free of the ordinary calamities and changes. Their windows are never darkened, they buy no graves, no hearse stands at their door, tears never stain their faces. God holds back desolating grief from them, yet He is never thanked. The monotony of their life does not bring repentance. They take a sheltered life as a matter of course.

But stagnant waters become putrid. Summer heat breeds obnoxious insects. To be without trouble can mean that one is without God.

THE LESSONS OUR CHANGES TEACH

Life's changes should aways lead us nearer to God. Jacob thought all his adversaries were against him, but he came to see that they were stepping stones to marvelous experiences.

What are some of the lessons we learn from the many upheavals in our lives? There is, first of all, *the sovereignty of God.*

God's purpose runs through all the changes in our lives. All the varied threads are in the hands of the Perfect Weaver. When severe change comes into our lives—when life is emptied of treasures, hopes, and ambitions—the first reaction of our agony is to think that God is cruel. But upon calmer reflection we withdraw our hard feelings and tell Him that He does all things well. Sorrow may be a road we don't look for, but it brings us to an appreciation of Romans 8:28. Upheavals in our lives ultimately prove that His Kingdom rules over all.

Then there is *the unchangeableness of God.* David knew that in spite of all the changes in his life, God Himself was unchanging in His character, purpose, and love. The writer of Hebrews says that "Jesus Christ is the same yesterday, today, and forever" (Heb. 13:8). Dr. Joseph Parker has it, "If God were always performing some conjuring trick on the battlements of heaven, the attention of the universe might be called to Him." But because of a certain monotony in God, men do not fear Him as they should.

We may become discouraged if we look at each of our days *separately.* We must learn, however, not to look at one day crowned with abundant success and another shadowed with trial and failure. Rather we must view all our days together and see what a wonderful pageant they make. Sublime victory is ours when we realize that all our days with all their changes have resulted in our becoming more like the Unchangeable One.

THE PERILS OF A LIFE WITHOUT CHANGE

Perhaps David's message regarding the perils of a changeless life has never really gripped us. But are there perils to fear in such a life? Yes, dangers there are, and may we be spared them by God's keeping power!

Hardness of heart

One of the greatest blessings of life is a tender heart. To be without love for God or man is indeed tragic. A person cannot effectively serve a world of need if he lacks sympathy. No one can understand the sorrows of others if he has been perpetually preserved from trials of his own. Such a person will become an unfeeling critic. He does not see why there should be so much suffering in the world. Why is he constantly pestered with appeals for help?

If the world were made up only of those people who have no change in their lives, no tragedies, and who, consequently, are past feeling, the world would be a cold place to live in. Thank God it is otherwise! Those who have experienced the school of grief and have been refined in the crucible of change are therefore able to exercise the ministry of comfort. No hands are so gentle as those that have known affliction. Hearts bleeding over their own adversities are able to weep with other

On the Monotony of Daily Life

grief-stricken souls. Men in sorrow seek out those who have also passed through the shadows. Jesus is able to aid those who are tempted, seeing He was tempted in all points as we are, yet without sin.

The neglect of eternity

A life without change is apt to make one materialistic. People who have much of this world's goods will live *for* them as well as *in* them. Any thought of the future is unwelcome because their lives are happy, uninterrupted ones. Circumstances for them are never altered or disturbed, and consequently their affections are set on earthly things. They have no desire to see God. Because the sufferings of this world have not come their way, there is little desire for heaven. They think they have everything they need here on earth.

Where do we stand in all this? What view of life is ours? Most of us do experience unexpected change, tragedy, and reversals at some time. Such change will oppress us if we look at our immediate life as an end in itself. Do we live only for present enjoyments, scorning the disturbing, unwelcome change that reaches others? Are we blind to the fact that the upheavals in our lives can ennoble our character, that we can become more like God by the path of pain? If this is our outlook, then we are not among the victorious army who bless the world.

If, on the other hand, we have learned how to make changes minister to us—if loss has yielded us gain, if poverty has given us wealth—then ours is a blessed life indeed. We are victorious when we know that all the unsettling changes that derange our schemes and destroy our pleasure but serve to remind us that we have no continuing city in this world of change. We must not be sad at being driven away from the security of this world, but rejoice at being driven into the arms of our Savior. When sorrow plunges deep into heart and home, it is blessed to know that in all of life's drastic changes, He who changes not is always near to cause all things to work together for good.

Chapter 7

THE GIFT OF TEARS

The apostle John's revelation of a world without tears is given twice in the last book of the Bible. ". . . God will wipe away every tear from their eyes . . ." (Rev. 7:17; 21:4). These words, unequalled in their depth and tenderness, are the same in both passages and relate to the same people. Yet the application of each passage is different, for each is speaking of a different period of time.

The first reference describes the condition of consolation in the Millennium. When Christ is here in person, reigning for a thousand years, no one will weep. As in the days of His flesh He banished tears, so there will be no sinning and sighing and sorrow when He appears.

The mention of a tearless world in Revelation 21 describes the eternal condition of consolation. An ocean of tears will flood the earth at the close of the Millennium. But with the removal of all causes of sorrow at the final Judgment, tears will forever vanish. Truly this is a glorious expectation for the believer. We should long for the day of Christ's return which will set in motion the events leading to His millennial reign and the banishment of our tears.

However, in the world, tears are common to all. The strongest, most joyful, or seemingly hard and thoughtless have those times when their faces are wet with tears. And surely there is nothing unmanly or unwomanly in the shedding of tears. Tears relieve burdened hearts and crushed spirits. Often we feel better after a crisis when we have had a good cry. Jesus wept! And His tears make Him sacred to our memory and have forever sanctified our tears and anguish.

Tears! Who can define them? They are agony in solution, liquid pain, watery anguish, heart-fluid. The message before us is that although we live in a world of broken hearts and although God did not promise that we would have no tears, He did say that our weeping can be victorious.

THE TEARS WE SHED

The eye is the fountain of sorrow, and various experiences of life cause the fountain to well up and send forth its stream of tears.

Doubtless when John penned his beautiful lines, he had Isaiah's description of a tearless world in mind: ". . . the Lord GOD will wipe away tears from off all faces . . ." (Is. 25:8). John does not tell us in this passage what heaven is like. But the apostle does contrast it with our lives here on earth. He cites an array of occasions for shedding tears as a contrast to the positive peace of God's people in eternity.

Here we have tears, misery, sickness, pain, and graves. God did not promise us freedom from such sorrows. His keeping power draws us to Himself, and He frequently uses pain to accomplish His ends. But in heaven we will be in intimate and constant communion with Him. We will have no need of being drawn closer.

And so over there we will experience the absence of all the causes of anguish, as well as the addition of a glorious provision of unending bliss. In eternity there will be no more death, no more sorrow, no more pain, and no more crying.

NO MORE DEATH!

Death never leaves dry eyes behind! Who does not weep before the coming of such a tyrant? The death of His friend Lazarus caused Jesus to weep.

Physical death fills this world with tears, for it is hard to say good-bye. For each of us the day comes when we have to lay some corpse to rest. No graves, however, are to be dug in heaven. Once the last enemy is destroyed permanently, cemeteries will be unknown. What a happy world this would be if death could be banished! More tears are shed over the partings of loved ones than anything else you care to mention. But the prospect of dry eyes, happy hearts, and unbroken fellowship is presented by John. "There shall be no more death, . . . for the former things have passed away."

Spiritual death likewise produces tears, for Jesus wept not only over Lazarus but over Jerusalem. He shed tears for lost souls who were spiritually dead while they were physically alive. Whether physical or spiritual death causes our tears, we can say with Christina Rossetti:

> *All tears are done away*
> *with the bitter unquiet sea;*
> *Death done away from among the living*
> *at last;*

Man shall say of sorrow—
Love granted it to thee and me!—
At last—It is past.

NO MORE SORROW!

The word John uses for sorrow in Revelation 21:4 is akin to that used in Revelation 18:15 where we read of weeping and wailing—a severe sorrow. Tears of sorrow are common to humanity. They reveal themselves in many ways and have many causes. Let us trace the common causes of such liquid pain.

Sorrow because of our sin

Who has never wept over his own failure and imperfections? Our lives are crippled by the forces wrapped up in our evil nature, and it brings us great sorrow. Only the unregenerate man has never turned aside from his sinful deeds and wept for a cleaner heart, a holier life, a deeper, fuller consecration.

We are living in a contaminated atmosphere in which it is becoming more difficult to remain unworldly. But the time is coming when we will be as absolutely holy as Christ is. Tears will never be shed over personal shortcomings. Now we bemoan our sin. John, however, stirs us with the hope that all such tears are to be wiped away. Holy lives and tearless eyes are to be ours when Jesus comes.

Sorrow because of a sinning world

The devilish intrusion of sin into God's fair universe has flooded the world with tears. Jesus beheld the city of Jerusalem and wept over it. His heart was broken because of the sin and stubbornness He saw in the lives of others. Do we manifest the passion of the Master? Have we become hardened to the evil in the world around us, or do we weep at the sin and shortcomings of those we meet? The more we become like God's dear Son, the more sin will break our hearts. In eternity a world without sin will be a world without sorrow and tears.

Sorrow because of ill-treatment

Reproach broke the heart of Christ. The cruel treatment by His professed friends brought about His death. His deepest wounds were caused by the Jews, Judas, and His own disciples.

All of us have friends who give us pain. We have scars that friendly hands have caused. But life's disappointments and ill-treatment cause us to rely on the One who is unfailing and unchanging in His goodness and friendship. When others cause us pain, we can let that pain fester inside us, building hatred and resentment. But we are only hurting ourselves. Instead we can remember the example of Christ who wept for the sins of others. John, however, tells us of a world without tears made possible because there will be no mistreatment of one person by another. No tears will flow because of the unloving attitude of others. We will live together without a single shadow to cross life's sky.

But until we reach that blissful time, may we be saved from causing unnecessary tears. Let us not consciously add to the sorrows of the world. Let us strive to be more kind, loving, thoughtful. There are many tears we can wipe away, and drying tears is a God-like occupation.

Sorrow because of the trials of life

All around there are those with blighted hopes and frustrated desires. Cherished plans sometimes burst like bubbles in the air. Experiences costing many tears and heartaches have to be faced. Parents weep over a much loved child who has turned from the Lord. A widow weeps over her husband taken from her side. The businessman weeps when the tide goes against him, and he is nearly broken with despair. How crestfallen he is as he looks at his castles in ruins at his feet.

But before long such tears will be wiped away. Tennyson's beautiful sentence comes to mind: "That made me count the less of sorrows when I caught a glimpse of the sorrowless Eternity." Have you caught a glimpse of this sorrowless eternity? ". . . The LORD shall give thee rest from thy sorrow . . ." (Is. 14:3). What healing balm this is for stricken hearts! All tears of sorrow are to be wiped away.

NO MORE PAIN!

John says, ". . . there shall be no more pain, . . ." implying *all* pain, no matter how it is caused. The word includes all painful labor and weariness as well as physical pain. How stricken with pain the human race is! We experience mental and physical pain. We experience sickness and war. Truly a man is born to trouble as the sparks fly upward. Some are born sickly. They never enjoy health. Entering the world, they suffer all their days. Others are beset by plagues, fevers, mental and physical maladies.

The promise of a world without pain, however, is the hope of all those who are patiently enduring a long night of suffering. No pain, no pangs—what a paradise! In a land of pure delight, pleasure is to banish pain. John 11, which tells of the death and resurrection of Lazarus, gives a picture of a world of sickness, pain, sorrows, tears, graves. John 12, which tells of the supper at Bethany and our Lord's triumphal entry into Jerusalem, finds tears and partings all banished and loved ones reunited. And how we long for bodies perfectly healthy and holy.

NO MORE CRYING!

No more death! No more sorrow! No more pain! Without these burdens of our present world, the apostle can promise us that there will be no more crying. The word John uses for "crying" implies a voice of despair, a loud outcry, groans similar to those associated with the strong crying of Hebrews 5:7. In Gethsemane the Master wept in anguish. Thus it is with ourselves. Sitting in the shadows, we cry over the unexplained experiences of life, we sigh for an explanation of our tears. But not until we reach heaven will we read the meaning of our darkest hours. Then there will be no more crying.

THE DIVINE HANDKERCHIEF

No wonder Robert Burns, the Scottish poet, was affected as he read this lovely promise that "God shall wipe away every tear from their eyes." He was always deeply moved as he thought upon God's hand as the handkerchief waiting to dry all human tears. It should be noted that in both Revelation 7:17 and Revelation

The Keeping Power of God

21:4 the drying is ascribed to God and not to the Lamb. The reason is that all sin, which is the root of all tears, is committed first of all against God. Because He is the greatest sufferer, He removes all the causes of the tears upon your face and mine.

God will be able to give us tearless eyes, seeing that the Devil, death and hell are all in the Lake of Fire, the final depository of all the roots of sorrow. A new world is to be ushered in, in which no one is to weep. This old world, the scene of sin, sorrow, and suffering is to be transformed into a tearless Eden.

Who would not shed life's tears when God's hand waits to wipe them away? So let us take comfort from John's blessed word. Now tears are with us day and night, and we should use the experiences that cause our tears to draw us closer to God. But John foresaw that day when all tears will be dried by the hand that will lead and feed us forever. What a victory for God and the redeemed! A land without graves, groans, and grief. May we all share it! May God hasten the fulfillment of His own promise and grant us a world without tears!

Chapter 8

WHAT TO DO WITH WORRY

What a world of worry ours is! Worry is driving people mad and is largely responsible for the alarming increase of depression and suicide. Trouble, anxiety, and vexations of mind characterize our life, and worrying seems to be the most common and natural thing to do. Yet it is the most useless, unnecessary, and harmful way out of our anguish. Worry can whiten the hair before time, fill a life with misery, fatten the doctor's purse, and extract an almost greater toll of life than all the physical diseases put together. Let us thank God that He can keep us even from worry. Jesus came that we might have peace.

THE CAUSE OF WORRY

As a gifted physician strives to get at the root cause of a disease before applying an efficacious remedy, so let us examine some of the sources responsible for the worry robbing our lives of peace and pleasure. Of this we are confident: There is no reason why so many people should live in the dark shadows where fears haunt them like ghosts.

The cares of life

Home cares, business, health, money matters, and loved ones are the cause of a great deal of worry. Every fluctuating, threatening circumstance is a signal for fresh indulgence of worry. But there is an important lesson in the motto, "Don't worry. It may not happen." What we seem to forget is that worry, when once formed as a personal habit, is difficult to check. Like ruts in a road that become deeper with use, so worry makes inroads upon our own and others' happiness. A good slogan to keep before us is:

Why worry about tomorrow?
It is always a day away.

The atmosphere of the world

Often we worry because others worry. Like a fever, worry is contagious. Worry is of the world, and it is very easy to fall into a worldly way of looking at things. The world worries, and it has every right to because it is away from God. Christians, however, breathe a different atmosphere and should be free from the way of the world. A Christian should segregate himself from those who are overtaken by the worries of this world just as he would segregate himself from a person with a contagious fever.

Ignorance of God

Another evident reason for worry is ignorance regarding the exact nature of God and His care. The person who worries fails to grasp the reality of a living heavenly Father. He is not appropriated as "the hidden source of calm repose." We forget that while there is need of grace there is also always grace for need.

Jesus corrects unnecessary anxiety when He tells us not to worry about tomorrow. Of course, He does not mean that we are to have no provident thought, such as when we put something aside for a rainy day. Not to do so is to be worse than an infidel, Paul reminds us. What our Lord had in mind was a carefree life made possible by the surrender of each day and its needs into the hands of our bountiful Father above. When troubled about food, clothes, and other necessities, we are to remember the birds and flowers. God feeds and clothes them, and He will provide our needs as well.

THE CURSE OF WORRY

Worry is never a blessing, but always a bane; never a comfort, but always a curse. It is senseless and foolish as can be demonstrated by its harm to ourselves, its harm to others, and its harm to God. These three reasons also indicate why, if we are His, we should not be guilty of the sin of worry.

Harmful to ourselves

Worrying never changes our circumstances in the least degree. As our Lord expressed it, anxiety cannot add one cubit to our stature. How can worry possibly benefit those who indulge in it?

Worry ruins one mentally, physically, and spiritually. A load of care or anxiety on the mind upsets the digestion process, produces undernourishment, and thereby makes one unfit for the responsibilities of life. Worry deranges the nervous system, robs a person of sleep, and often causes heavy doctor's bills. Doctors, however, can do little for one who worries. The only cure, as we shall later see, is a right relationship with God.

Harmful to others

One who worries displays a depressed feeling and, as mentioned before, worry and depression are contagious. It is harmful and annoying to have around us those who rob us of our joy. Therefore worrying is harmful not only to the person who is worrying, but to those he infects as well.

There is another more serious aspect to the way in which worry is harmful to others. If we are the Lord's, we must realize that the world waits to see how we are affected by our trials and losses. When our heart is robbed of some treasure, how do we act? If we worry and mope, lose heart, and go to pieces as if we had no source of strength, those around us have every right to doubt the reality of our faith and of God's care. Our worry may affect the eternal destiny of others. It is imperative for the sake of others to let the peace of God rule in our hearts when sorrows and adversities overtake us.

Harmful to God

A worrying Christian contradicts the sufficiency of divine grace and damages the reputation of God as a Father who really cares. When such a mental habit is practiced, we proclaim to others that God is not able to care for us as He promised to do. Worry sends off deadly gases, destructive to faith. Fretful doubt obscures God's face. Worry certainly hurts His loving heart. It must grieve the Lord to know that although He is almighty and beneficent, His children persist in worrying over little things. Faith in times of difficulty pleases and honors Him.

> *When worrying we are not trusting,*
> *When trusting, we are not worrying.*

Worry demonstrates doubt in a threefold direction:

1. God's *love* is doubted. Worry implies that He cares little for His blood-washed children.
2. God's *wisdom* is doubted. Worry indicates that He is not able to plan for His own, that He does not know what is best for those who belong to Him.
3. God's *power* is doubted. Worry declares that His grace is not sufficient for our needs, that His keeping power is turned off.

The spirit of worry is calamitous. A surgeon knowing something of the peril of this sin had placed in his office the words, "Don't worry—it is wicked." And wicked it is! Many who agree that worry is a useless, senseless habit are nevertheless slow to admit that it is a sin. And yet, ". . . whatever is not from faith is sin" (Rom. 14:23). God has promised to care for us at all times. Our worry, however, makes Him out a liar. Whittier's beautiful lines are a corrective to the tendency to worry and doubt:

> *I know not where His islands lift*
> *Their fronded palms in air,*
> *I only know I cannot drift*
> *Beyond His love and care.*

THE CURE OF WORRY

If there is a life without worry, surely all of us will want to know and experience such a carefree existence. If there is a cure for this ravaging disease, then we should proclaim it near and far in this troubled, worry-driven world.

Unfortunately, there are those suffering under this slow form of self-inflicted suicide who believe that it is possible to alleviate worry merely by wishing it away. Mind, they say, influences matter. The teacher asks if the seeker is worrying about anything. If the answer is "yes" then the advice is, "Well, stop it! Go out and smile and be resolved never to worry again." But such a source of relief does not work.

The word *worry*, we are informed, is from an Anglo-Saxon term meaning "a wolf," an animal who harasses and harms. If such a wolf as worry is to be destroyed, it will never be by our own power or self-thought. Unless the Lion of Judah takes it in hand to destroy our troubling cares, then we are without hope. Thank God, there is relief for those who are harried by the wolf! Would you have a life without worry and victory over lurking fears? Here are the ingredients in God's keeping power over worry.

Peace through trusting

The miracle of being without worry in this modern age is a miracle the Holy Spirit makes possible through the impartation of a divine peace. With a mind in tune with the Lord, we can be kept in the experience of a continuous, uninterrupted peace (see Is. 26:3).

Unfortunately, we too often know Jesus only as our

sin-bearer but not as our burden-bearer. We give Him
our sins but not our worries. We fix our minds on trouble, rather than on the Lord. Our difficulties are magnified, and the Master's grace is belittled. But when the
reverse process is practiced, and the goodness of the
Lord fills our mind, then the things of earth grow
strangely dim. We can sing with Frances Ridley
Havergel:

> *Hidden in the hollow of His blessed hand,*
> *Never foe can follow, never traitor stand.*
> *Not a surge of worry, not a shade of care,*
> *Not a blast of hurry, touch the Spirit there.*
> *Stayed upon Jehovah, hearts are fully blest,*
> *Finding as He promised, perfect peace and rest.*

Peace through loving

Another sword effective in the slaughter of the wolf
of worry is to be found in Romans 8:28, where we discover that if we love God, then all things, even the
unpleasant experiences of life, work together for good.
Things not good in themselves can, under the hand of
God, produce peace of heart. The love of God stands
between us and all possible harm. Therefore our love of
God can rest in the joy of His ability to undertake for us
even in whatever dark hours we may face.

Peace by casting

Peter gives us another avenue of victory over worry
and fear. An appealing translation of his exhortation
has been stated, "Casting all your care upon Him, for it
matters to Him about you" (1 Pet. 5:7.) Dr. Weymouth's

interpretation of this passage is likewise suggestive, "Throw the whole of your anxiety upon Him because He, Himself, cares for you." If we trust some of our care to Him, why not let Him have it all?

Sometimes we find ourselves saying that we are happy, "under the circumstances." But as Christians we have no right to be *under* our circumstances. We should be on the top of them, reigning over them with Christ.

Peace through looking

A right understanding of Hebrews 12:1,2 will bring peace to careworn hearts. We are to look away from all else and turn our eyes to Jesus. Not a glance but a gaze. The Master is able to keep us in perfect peace, seeing that He faced every kind of test and emerged conqueror. Nothing ever disturbed Him. He could never be robbed of His spiritual possession of tranquility as an antidote of worry and despair.

Peace through protection

In Philippians 4:6,7,19, Paul offers another corrective for the disturbing forces of life. We ought to be happy and free from worry because the Lord encamps around His own. He promises to protect our hearts and minds. Do you want to put off the wolf of worry? Well, look at this threefold weapon.

1. Be anxious for nothing. And nothing means *no thing*. Surely this excludes even the slightest reasons for unrest and disturbance of peace.

2. Be prayerful for everything. How different our lives would be if only we could adopt the prayer-

attitude as we come up against the difficult experiences of life! This is always the way of victory.

3. Be grateful in all things. We are told that "my God shall supply all your need according to His riches in glory by Christ Jesus." The Lord supplied Paul's needs, and He will supply ours as well. His goodness extends from the time we first meet Him until we go home to be with Him. And with such a bountiful God, why would we burden our souls with worries and cares?

Do you live on "Thanksgiving Avenue"? The houses are no more expensive than they are on "Worry Street." Pack up and leave such a gloomy quarter where the sun seldom shines. The next time you are tempted to sit and brood, take a pencil and put down a list of all the mercies you enjoy, and then say to your soul, "Why are you cast down? . . . / Hope in God, / For I shall yet praise Him" (Ps. 43:5).

Chapter 9

AT WITS' END CORNER

In his graphic description of a ship thrown about by stormy winds, the psalmist refers to the crew as being at their wits' end (Ps. 107:27). Surely the language used by the psalmist is as sublime as the message is compelling.

The psalmist's desire is "that men would give thanks to the LORD for His goodness" (Ps. 107:31). "Those who go down to the sea in ships," he says, ". . . see the works of the LORD" (vv. 23,24) in the power of the sea during a storm. Winds and waves roar. The sea tosses the ship about as a plaything. Crews, thrown into confusion and unable to steer their ships to port, pray to heaven for deliverance from distress and perplexity. God's power is again shown as He calms the storm and ". . . guides them to their desired haven. Oh, that men would give thanks to the LORD for His goodness,/And for His wonderful works to the children of men!" (v. 31).

Such a vivid picture of a storm at sea reminds us of Jonah's experience, and, on a smaller scale, the fishermen in their boat on the Sea of Galilee with their precious cargo, the weary, sleeping Christ. It may be that Matthew had this Psalm in mind or in front of him as he recorded the stilling of the tempest by his Lord. "He calms the storm . . ." (Ps. 107:29) is reflected in Matthew's words, ". . . He arose . . . and there was a great calm" (Matt. 8:26).

However, the feeling of despair indicated by the striking phrase "at their wits' end" is what we want to consider. Certainly the sailor in a ship tossed about by huge waves has a feeling of helplessness that can lead to despair. Most of us have felt that kind of despair at one time or another. We feel as if we have no place to turn for help and are at our wits' end. But God's power is sufficient even in those moments. He will help us through the darkest times. Let us think of several who often feel such despair and should be ready to employ the keeping power of God.

THOSE WHO SEARCH AFTER TRUTH

The word *wit* comes from the Old English word *witan*, meaning "to know." There are many who are pressed with a sincere desire to understand the true import of spiritual things; yet they try to do so without the eye of faith, but with the mind of reason, and find themselves overwhelmed by doubt. In childhood, they had no doubts. The most mysterious things appeared simple. But with the passage of time they tried to reason out the mysteries of God, and certainties became uncertainties. Problems, which faith alone can accept, were dealt with by scientific processes. Now with baffled minds, these perplexed souls are at sea.

Such darkness of mind carries with it the danger of unbelief. Another way of translating the Hebrew for "at their wits' end" is "all their wisdom is swallowed up." What a striking picture of the hopelessness man feels when his wisdom can no longer help him. Trusting his own fleshly wisdom, he inevitably comes to his wits' end, not knowing what to believe. Human reasoning, he comes to discover, is unable to comprehend the dealings of God.

Such a searcher after truth may be sincere, but when the mind is tossed about by contrary winds, faith yields to doubt, doubt turns to despair, and despair may turn to agnosticism—that black midnight of unbelief. Recognizing the limitation of knowledge, Socrates confessed, "I know only that I know little or nothing at all." Our own wits, unaided by the Holy Spirit, can never penetrate the deep things of God and His Word. There are phases of the divine revelation we must accept by faith, and others we can only understand as heavenly wisdom is granted. We can be kept by the power of God when we rejoice in the hopelessness we may feel as all our fleshly wisdom is swallowed up. We come to the end of our own puny reasoning and by faith accept the spiritual understanding the Spirit makes possible.

THOSE CONFRONTED
WITH DIFFICULT TASKS

The apostle Paul hardly knew how to manage the Galatians. In despair he exclaimed, "I am at my wits' end about you" (Gal. 4:20 MOFFATT). Jonah is a classic illustration of a person who is confronted with a task which he does not want to perform or which he thinks is too difficult. He pondered God's command to go to Nineveh and "cry against it" and decided instead to run away. Rather than going to Nineveh, he paid his own fare to Tarshish, and having quieted his conscience he fell asleep. But when the storm broke, the shipmaster and crew were at their wits' end. In their dilemma, they proved to be the salvation of the Lord for Jonah by giving him a second opportunity to go to Nineveh.

A Spanish proverb says, "A storm at sea teaches us to pray." How true this is in the varied experiences of life. Sometimes we are brought into perplexing circumstances in which we know not what to do or where to turn for relief. Or it may be that we face a task we feel unable to tackle. In our despair we turn to the Lord. Those in the Psalm who were at their wits' end had *wit* enough to pray, for we read that ". . . they cry out to the Lord." The Lord will provide strength and comfort when we are in despair.

Prayer is good in a storm, but why wait until the storm before we pray? Stunned and staggering, we can turn to God and hear Him answer us out of the storm. In the whale's belly, Jonah cast his seemingly impossible situation upon the Lord. "He that cannot pray, let him go to sea and there he will learn." Overwhelming cares teach us how to cast every one of them upon the Lord.

Yet we err if we think that God is needed more in distress than in calm. In the spiritual realm, calm waters are more dangerous than rough seas, for they tempt us to rely on our own strength and wisdom rather than on God's power. It is true that our extremity is God's opportunity, but He also loves to have opportunities to display His power when the waters are tranquil.

THOSE IN TROUBLE

The majority of us have experienced those troubles and upheavals of life when, almost driven to despair, we have looked to heaven only to find it like brass. There seems to be no response. Yet a phrase like "grace to help in time of need" (Heb. 4:16) implies that in the very nick of time, never before or after our time of need, God is right there to strengthen, help, and bless us.

George Washington was a praying man. When he left home his mother said, "My son, never neglect the duty of secret prayer." And he never did. He would rise at 4:00 A.M. for devotions. Once, a Quaker walking in the creek near Valley Forge heard a voice in the thicket and found Washington on his knees with his face uplifted and his eyes full of tears. The new country's cause was in danger at the time. His troops were barefooted, hungry, and heartsick. The treasury was empty. But in his extremity he prayed and prevailed.

Thus it is with ourselves. Our extremities give God His opportunity. The despair we feel when we are in trouble lets Him demonstrate His keeping power. His strength is made perfect in our weakness. At the end of ourselves, we find God. When we are in a tight corner and at the end of our resources, there come surprises of divine grace and power.

THOSE FACING TEMPTATION

Doubts, fears, terrors, temptations, anxieties, like angry waves, wait to engulf us. When the storms and winds beat upon us and we are nearly ready to sink, we wonder what to do. No matter who we are, none of us will escape the hurricane of temptation. When it comes, possibly it will be with the realization of our utter inability to battle temptation in our own strength.

The picture drawn in Psalm 107 is that of the shipmaster's using every expedient known to navigation, but his ship is strained and tossed about like a cork and he does not know how to keep it afloat. Thus it is with ourselves when we face a sudden blast of satanic temptation and it seems as if we must go under altogether. God, however, is always at hand with His way of escape. At the opportune moment He reveals Himself as the God of deliverance.

THOSE UNDER CONVICTION OF SIN

Despair is sometimes felt when a consciousness of sin sweeps over the soul, gathering the force of a tempest. The exceeding sinfulness of sin is realized, and the mind is oppressed by the person's failure to bring glory to God and by the certainty of God's judgment. In utter despair and remorse, the helpless cry goes out, "What can I do?"

I pray that we could see multitudes at their wits' end in this respect, for conviction of sin is necessary before a person realizes his need of God. The prodigal son found himself without a crust of bread, and in desperation he came back to his father. If ever a man was at his wits' end, it was the dying thief. Yet after a life of sin and shame, he entered paradise after looking at Christ. The words of Isaiah reflect the desperation brought about by conviction of sin, which he felt after seeing the glory of God. ". . . Woe is me! for I am undone; because I am a man of unclean lips, and I dwell in the midst of a people of unclean lips . . ." (Is. 6:5).

Can it be that as you read these lines, you have a fear of judgment because of your load of sin? You tremble, knowing that the penalty of a violated law is death. The only way you can quit your sin is by the acceptance of Christ as your substitute. By His death He paid the penalty the sinner should have met, and now, as a lawyer pleading a case, He presents His finished work on the sinner's behalf.

If you are without Christ, will you not believe that He is your only hope of salvation? Will you not fling your exhausted life at the feet of this all-compassionate, all-pardoning Savior? By His agony and shame He calls you to cast yourself in all your helplessness upon His mercy.

THOSE FACING THE TERROR OF DEATH

Although we know that each of us will some day die, we frequently fear death. There is no need for a Christian to view death with despair, but unfortunately many do not claim God's promises at this point. Empty chairs, crushed hopes, human props giving way often drive us to our wits' end. In spite of the advance of knowledge, we find that science and human skill still stand helpless before the onward march of death.

Victory over the terror of death is the greatest battle God's keeping power can wage for us. Yet it will come only if we have been in the habit throughout our lives of appropriating the keeping power of God for small victories. A victorious stance throughout our lives will lead to a glorious victory at the end of it.

The Israelites were not a seafaring people. This is one reason why mariners were lauded for their daring and bravery. Their tales of the sea thrilled all hearts. Sailors were men of renown, who were listened to with reverent attention. One of the fascinations of heaven will be the testimonies of believers recounting how, after being at their wits' end many times, they were graciously borne over the waters of death. One of the chief wonders alluded to in Psalm 107 is the calm following a terrific, sudden storm. That is how it will be with ourselves, when after crossing the turbulent waters, we find ourselves in the haven of rest above.

Of course, we recognize that all believers have not the same experience. Some saints appear to have more soul trouble and heart anguish than others. Yet if in divine providence we sail over the deeps of inward depravity, or the waste waters of poverty, or the billows of persecution, or the rough waves of temptation, or the dark seas of death, all will be well if we have Christ as our pilot. With Him in full control of our little craft, we can sail into heavenly port with the flags of victory flying at full mast.

The victory over despair that we will know with finality and certainty in heaven can be ours daily if we rely not on our own resources, but on God's power. This victory over despair in the dark and difficult hours of life is beautifully expressed by Antoinette Wilson.

Wits' End Corner

Are you standing at "Wits' End Corner,"
Christian, with troubled brow?
Are you thinking of what is before you,
And all you are bearing now?
Does all the world seem against you,
And you in the battle alone?
Remember, at Wits' End Corner,
Is just where God's power is shown.

At Wits' End Corner

Are you standing at "Wits' End Corner"
   Blinded with wearying pain
Feeling you cannot endure it
   You cannot bear the strain;
Bruised through the constant suffering,
   Dizzy, and dazed, and numb?
Remember, to Wits' End Corner
   Is where Jesus loves to come!

Are you standing at Wits' End Corner,
   Your work before you spread,
All lying begun, unfinished,
   And pressing on heart and head,
Longing for strength to do it,
   Stretching out trembling hands?
Remember—at Wits' End Corner
   The Burden Bearer stands.

Are you standing at Wits' End Corner,
   Yearning for those you love,
Longing and praying and watching,
   Pleading their cause above?
Trying to lead them to Jesus,
   Wondering if you've been true?
He whispers at Wits' End Corner
   "I'll win them, as I won you!"

Are you standing at Wits' End Corner?
   Then you're just at the very spot
To learn the wondrous resources
   Of Him who faileth not!
No doubt to a brighter pathway
   Your footsteps will soon be moved,
But only at Wits' End Corner
   Is "the God Who is able" proved!

Chapter 10

A LOOK AT LONELINESS

F. W. Robertson of Brighton, England, whose masterly sermons ought to be read by every preacher, has a unique chapter in one of his books, the *Loneliness of Christ*, in which he indicates that there are two kinds of solitude.

There is what he calls *insulation in space*, that is, separation caused by distance. But this kind of solitude does not necessarily cause loneliness of the heart, for the memory of friends and loved ones can people our solitude with a crowd. A missionary in some lonely outpost is not lonely as he thinks of loving, praying friends who constantly remember his needs.

Then there is *isolation of the spirit*, or loneliness of the soul. Paul was left in the crowded city of Athens—alone. One can feel lonely even in the heart of a crowd. Some of the most lonely people today live in some of the largest cities. F. W. Robertson then shows that people respond to loneliness in two different ways.

First, self-reliant, self-dependent, some people are firm and unbending, strongly determined to face their duty alone. They never dread unpopularity and reproach. They crave no sympathy for their isolation. Elijah, alone in the wilderness when the court deserted him, dared sternly to face the false prophets of Baal alone.

The other kind of people are those who must have sympathy and friendship. They tremble at the thought of being left alone, not because they lack courage but solely because of the intensity of their affection. Jacob, left alone, slept on his way to Padan-aram on the first night away from under his father's roof. The sympathy he yearned for, however, came in a dream. The Lord Jesus Christ also sought friendship and not only gave sympathy, but yearned for it. "Do you also want to go away?" A stern, hard spirit would never say, ". . . I am not alone, because the Father is with Me" (John 16:32).

A GALLERY OF LONELY SOULS

The Bible contains many biographies of lonely men and women. Solitude is the narrow gate the majority of the redeemed must pass through.

Abel was murdered alone. He was a man who sacrificed the firstlings of his flock to the Lord, and he died a lonely death for his creed.

Noah watched the threatening clouds of judgment alone. His vision and prophecy of the flood were not shared by others. In his genealogy he is spoken of as the only man perfect in his generation.

Abraham, obedient to the will of God, offered to sacrifice his beloved son of promise on Mount Moriah—alone.

Jacob wrestled with God alone. His name and nature were changed after he sent his wives ahead and "he was left alone."

Joseph, before he could act and reign as the savior of Egypt, had to suffer in the pit of rejection—alone.

Moses, in order to give Israel a revelation of God, had to climb Mount Sinai and face God—alone.

David achieved his victory over Goliath—alone. His confidence in God was unshared by any of the men in the army of Israel.

Esther cried, "If I perish, I perish," as she sought the presence of the king—alone.

Daniel, in order to display the power of God, had to meet the hungry lions—alone. And "left alone" he received the glorious vision of the divine program of the ages.

The disciples, who longed to teach the mysteries of the kingdom, had to get with Jesus—alone.

Paul, before he could bring the gospel to Rome, the center of the then-known world, had to defy Caesar—alone.

John, before he could write the soul-thrilling apocalypse of Christ's final triumph over all evil forces, had to be left on Patmos—alone.

The life of Jesus is particularly impressive because of its solitude. He had experiences He could never share with others. Because He was the Son of God, He had to be alone. The divine elevation of His character gave Him a loneliness unshared by men. When He was but twelve years old, He was left by His parents in Jerusalem. He was separated from this family because His parents could not understand His high thoughts and divine vocation. From His lonely soul came the question, "Did you not know that I must be about My Father's business?" (Luke 2:49).

Loneliness was likewise faced in His Nazareth home, for those around Him did not believe in Him. Yet His was not the solitariness of a lonely hermit. It was the isolation of the spirit.

Gethsemane was another experience Christ tasted alone. There was no sorrow like His sorrow. He had to tread the winepress alone. Every person must face the hour of trial alone. Everyone must bear his own burden. There are some experiences we can never share with others. No stranger dare interfere with the agony of your soul.

Calvary found Jesus alone. His disciples had forsaken Him, and although two thieves shared the form of His death, He was alone in His anguish. Yes, and in that dark, lone hour He was made to bear the extreme limit of loneliness. " 'My God, My God, why have *You* forsaken Me?' " (Matt. 27:46, italics added).

> *Alone, alone, He bore it all alone,*
> *He gave Himself to save His own,*
> *He suffered, bled, and died, alone, alone.*

THE ISOLATION CONSECRATION PRODUCES

Solitude is therefore not necessarily a condition to be avoided. We have seen how many of the men and women of God in Scriptures have been alone. But we must be careful. To be wrapped up in ourselves, to become loveless, unsympathetic, cold, unobliging, indifferent to the welfare and needs of others, to live in a little world of our own, is to produce a fruitless solitude. People will leave us very much alone if we live unto ourselves. Such self-centeredness produces a loneliness caused by our personality, not by our walk with the Lord.

On the other hand, there is a loneliness we cannot avoid if we are fully identified with the lonely Christ. The world has little sympathy for divine holiness. Spirituality is very disagreeable to unspiritual people. We can still expect reproach from those who do not belong to the Savior. So, my friend, you are in good company if you are spurned, cut off, made to feel that you are not wanted, simply because of your allegiance to Christ. "Do not marvel, my brethren, if the world hates you" (1 John 3:13).

The Lord invites you to share His loneliness in a world in which He found rejection. Ponder these aspects of our relationship with Him.

1. We are called and blessed alone. ". . . I called him alone, and blessed him . . ." (Is. 51:2). In the hour we first come to God, God deals with us alone. There are no two spiritual experiences exactly alike. God deals with us as individuals. Therefore, let us never try to force another into our own mold.

2. We are led and guided alone. "The LORD alone did lead him . . ." (Deut. 32:12). Often when making a deci-

sion, we are influenced by our own desires or by the persuasion of others. Oh, that we might be led of God no matter how such divine guidance may conflict with our own plans or the advice of others!

3. We suffer and weep alone. "He sitteth alone and keepeth silence . . ." (Lam. 3:28). "I lie awake . . . like a sparrow alone on the housetop" (Ps. 102:7). There are tears, sorrows, and separations we cannot share with others. In Gethsemane Christ cried out to God alone, and He suffered and died alone on Golgotha. So it must be with our lives.

4. We must be content to serve alone. "Lord, do You not care that my sister has left me to serve alone?" (Luke 10:40). If others leave us high and dry because of our spiritual principles and methods, we must realize that such rejection is part of the price of our identification with Christ. Paul offers an encouraging contrast in 2 Timothy 4. When he was brought to trial, ". . . no one stood with me . . . ," he laments. "But," he says, "the Lord stood with me and strengthened me. . . ." Divine companionship was his.

5. We have to prevail with God alone. Jesus went apart to pray and was there alone (see Matt. 14:23). Christ urges us to shut the door and get alone with God. What do we know of this aloneness? Are we too much in the company of others? The fellowship of saints, blessed though it be, must never be substituted for deep, personal communion with God. Such solitude produces a fuller revelation. "I was left alone, and saw this great vision . . ." (Dan. 10:8). In such solitariness our witness is that one with God is always the majority.

THE BLESSEDNESS OF SPIRITUAL SOLITUDE

Alone, we are never lonely. It is the blessed privilege of every child of God to abide in living union with the living Christ. ". . . I am not alone, because the Father is with Me" (John 16:32). Is it not blessed to know that we have the joy of sharing heaven's companionship?

We will never experience the dread of isolation that our Savior did when He cried on Calvary, "My God, My God, why have You forsaken Me?" Those words will never be repeated by us, because we have the promise, ". . . I will never leave you nor forsake you" (Heb. 13:5).

We have the company of the Father: ". . . My Father will love him, and We will come to him and make our home with him" (John 14:23). We have the fellowship of the Son: ". . . behold, I am with you always . . ." (Matt. 28:20). We have the presence of the Holy Spirit: ". . . He may abide with you forever" (John 14:16). With such a blessed and blissful companionship, why should we be lonely or long for other friendship? If the circle of our acquaintances is becoming narrower and our so-called friends drop us because of our witness to the greatness and goodness of God, let us not mourn over our solitude. Victory will be ours if we can sing with May Grimes,

> *A little sanctuary art Thou to me!*
> *I am always "at home" on land or sea;*
> *Alone, yet never lonely now, I prove*
> *The "hundredfold," Lord Jesus, in Thy Love.*

Another has described God's keeping power over solitude in the precious lines,

> *Alone, yet not alone am I*
> *Though in this solitude so drear;*
> *I feel my Savior always nigh,*
> *He comes the weary hour to cheer;*
> *I am with Him, and He with me*
> *Even here alone I cannot be.*

Chapter 11

BY THIS SIGN CONQUER

Most of the conditions on which we have been meditating have been personal ones. God's mercy and power save us—a fact we will enjoy throughout eternity—but they also keep us while we are struggling on this earth with our old natures. God's mercy and power keep us from sin, temptation, monotony, sorrow, worry, and loneliness. But God is not limited to our personal conditions. His power is over all. His sovereignty extends throughout the whole earth.

It is both refreshing and inspiring in these days of global power struggles and crumbling earthly governments to return to the Psalms, with their air of certainty regarding the present sovereignty and coming universal dominion of the Lord. Psalm 96 portrays God's supremacy as being unchallenged in every realm.

For a summary of this theocratic Psalm we turn to verse 10, which presents a threefold cord of sovereignty, security, and sanctity that cannot be broken.

SOVEREIGNTY

"Say among the nations,/'The LORD reigns. . . . ,'" This is an age of proud political dictators. Man has little room for God. Brute force appears to be the world's sovereign lord, yet amid chaos, despair, and godlessness, God reigns!

God is not dead, as some would believe. He may appear to be standing in the wings. His throne, however, has not been abdicated. This guilty earth will yet receive His reckoning, for He is sovereign.

SECURITY

". . . The world also is firmly established,/It shall not be moved. . . ." To our eyes there appears to be little semblance of this predicted, settled order. We live in a changing world. Thrones, governments, and systems are changing with startling rapidity. Nothing is firmly established. But this verse offers us a changeless world, an order of government fixed and immovable. Such a condition will be experienced by us in the kingdom to come. Knowing that God is in control now, even of our changing world, offers us security.

SANCTITY

". . . He shall judge the peoples righteously." Here again we have a study in contrasts. Righteous judgment is a scarce commodity. Deceit, bribery, graft, corruption, and unrighteous practices are all associated with men and places least suspected.

In the decade of the seventies, some of the most powerful men in United States history were deposed from their governmental duties. Yes, the most influential of men are still only men. But a Man is coming, a glorified Man, who will judge the people righteously.

The theme of this meditation is that the Lord is in fact King. His power is not just over our personal conditions, but over the political and economic powers of the world. This theme is found in the first phase of verse 10: "Say among the nations,/'The LORD reigns . . .' "

Psalm 96 is a great missionary Psalm, for it reveals ancient Israel's responsibility to make God known among the nations, with emphasis to be placed upon the world empire of the heavenly Sovereign. God is declared an Emperor. There is, of course, a distinction between king and emperor. A king is the chief ruler in and over a nation. An emperor, however, is the highest title of sovereignty and suggests a ruler of nations and of lesser sovereigns. The day is coming when the kingdoms of this world will become a world-kingdom, and Christ will reign supreme over all (see Rev. 11:15).

Our English versions of verse 10 end with "the LORD reigns." But an old Latin version includes the words, "reigns from the tree." Justin Martyr accused the Jews of erasing the words "from the tree" from the original because of their intense hatred of Jesus, who is praised within the Psalm as Messiah. Through the centuries the verse was cherished as a prediction of the cross, but it was rejected as such by the Jews of the first two or three centuries. Thus all crucifixes before the eleventh century portrayed Christ as robed and crowned.

Jesus came as a King, and the throne from which He reigns is not a gilded one, as are the thrones of earth, but the gory cross of Calvary. An old Latin hymn has it:

> *Fulfilled in all that David did*
> *In true prophetic song of old:*

"Amid the nations God," saith he,
"Hath reigned and triumphed from the tree."

The truth, then, we are setting out to state is that Christ is sovereign King over all. The cross is His throne. The dying Savior was the triumphant Lord. He died as a victor, not a victim.

> *The truth that David learned to sing*
> *Its deep fulfillment here attains;*
> *Tell all the earth the Lord is King!*
> *Lo, from a cross a King He reigns.*

John Ellerton's lines suggest a similar thought:

> *Throned upon the awful Tree,*
> *King of Grief, I watch with Thee.*

Let us, then, meditate on the cross of Calvary and divine sovereignty.

The confession of sovereignty

"Say . . . 'The LORD reigns . . .' "

Divine sovereignty is a truth we need to experience personally and proclaim nationally. On every hand there is a tendency to deify man and humanize God. Let us therefore say, and utter it loudly, that God reigns!

Say it to the Kremlin, with its blatant godlessness and bloody rule, that God reigns and will yet laugh at those who try to exterminate Him.

Say it to Iran, proud and boastful nationally and corrupt religiously, that God reigns and will yet see to it that His Son will be fully worshiped and adored. Iran, with its hateful madness and pagan heresy, awaits divine judgment.

Say it to Britain, as it ignores God and righteousness and lives in the shadow of past glories, that God reigns and will hold a nation responsible if it once knew and proclaimed the truth and yet departed from it.

Say it to America, with its self-complacency, pornography, abortion on demand, and gross materialism, that God reigns and will yet exact the uttermost farthing in judgment.

Yes, and say it to our own hearts, when depressed by hostile forces arrayed against us, that God reigns! He rules over all! Glory to His name! The Lord God omnipotent reigns! Let the earth tremble. And it will tremble and crumble when His power is unleashed.

The circumference of sovereignty

". . . among the nations. . . ."

Divine sovereignty is not limited to the angelic realm or to a supernatural world we cannot feel and see. God's will is accomplished among the inhabitants of earth as well as with the army in heaven. All power is His in heaven and on earth.

God reigns among the nations! This is true even though the world bears no semblance of a divine rule. No matter where you look, truth seems to be on the scaffold and wrong seems to be on the throne. Strife, murder, hatred, chaos, and bloodshed are all around us. The world is an armed camp.

What kind of a world can we expect when Satan is its god? At present, the world is satanically controlled. Behind destructive engines of war, there is the destroyer. Chaos, anguish, blasted lives and hopes are caused by

Satan, who has been a murderer from the beginning. Our struggle is not against flesh and blood. One nation rises in the flesh and tries to conquer another nation prepared to fight back in the flesh. Earth's conflicts are not human, but superhuman and superterrestrial. We do not wrestle against flesh and blood but against the potentates of the dark present, the spiritual forces of evil in the heavenly sphere.

Yet, we are to proclaim among the nations, torn as they are by war and terrorism, that God reigns! No matter how the agony of the world may seem to contradict the truth of divine sovereignty, God is still able to make men and demons praise Him. God is supreme over Satan, over the nations, and over rulers. Hellish forces may appear to have the ascendancy, but the Devil who commands them is like a dog on a leash and cannot go beyond divine permission.

Our responsibility, then, is to declare among the nations that God's day is coming. Perplexed hearts feel that He is a little inactive, but He can afford to wait. He never acts before the time is right, nor is He ever behind schedule. God is coming to give the warring earth peace. He will yet reign without a rival. The uttermost parts of the earth will be His possession when, taking to Himself His undisputed power, He fashions the nations into His own world-kingdom.

The center of sovereignty

". . . from the tree. . . ."

This pregnant phrase is found in ancient translations and brings us to the secret and source of sovereignty. The cross provided Christ with the rights of kingship. If we understand the cross only in terms of the initial work of cleansing a sinner from the penalty and guilt of sin, we do not have a full understanding of the Scriptures. Calvary gave the Savior power over spheres as well as souls. By virtue of His anguish, shame, and sacrifice, Jesus will yet reign from shore to shore. The nail-pierced hand is to wield the scepter of universal dominion. John, in his apocalyptic vision, saw a slain Lamb conquering all hostile powers and establishing His worldwide reign.

Calvary, then, was a grim battlefield where Satan met his ultimate defeat, although God has allowed him to continue to have influence in this world. The cross was the bloody arena where Jesus laid hold of principalities, powers, world rulers, and satanic potentates and robbed them of their authority. When He cried, "It is finished," our Lord had in mind not only your redemption and mine, but the deliverance of a groaning world from the domination of Satan.

The cross, then, was a throne. From the tree, Jesus reigns over His own and will yet reign over the world. The cross transcends all human and hellish power. The blood of the Lamb made possible the sovereignty of the Lamb. The motto of an ancient Scottish house is a cross with the words: "By this sign we conquer." A cruel cross, then, will yet bring peace to this world. It will be a world in which the people shall ". . . beat their swords into plowshares, and their spears into pruning-hooks; nation shall not lift up sword against nation, neither shall they learn war any more" (Is. 2:4).

Yes, our adorable Lord reigns from His tree, and we must proclaim this truth to those nations that magnify and depend on brute force. At Calvary Jesus revealed how love can triumph over hate, unselfishness over greed, holiness over sin, truth over falsity, gentleness over force, sacrifice over sordid gain.

Chapter 12

PERSONAL WARS

In the last chapter we discussed global conflict and God's sovereignty throughout the whole earth. When warring nations declare an armistice and peace treaties are signed, millions of men are speedily demobilized. Because the conflict is over, they are discharged and allowed to return to their civilian lives and to more peaceful and secure occupations.

What a blissful world this would be if the peoples of the earth would quit their fighting! All of us would breathe more freely if we knew for sure that the world required soldiers no longer. But there will never be any discharge from bloody wars, skirmishes, and terrorist activity until Jesus comes to usher in His millennial reign.

The purpose of this chapter, however, is to discover some lessons on victory over personal wars which emerge from Solomon's declaration, ". . . there is no discharge in that war . . ." (Eccl. 8:8). We long for the day Christ will establish His millennial kingdom and thus bring perfect peace to the nations of the earth, but we recognize that wars and conflicts will be with us until then. In the same way, we long for the day we will reign with Christ and be free from our sinful nature, but we recognize that until then there are personal wars in which we are perpetually engaged and from which there is no discharge. Although death is the immediate enemy spoken of in this phrase from Ecclesiastes, the truth of Scripture lets us extend the application of the verse to other enemies as well. Here then are some of the foes assailing the peace of man from which we are kept as we appropriate the power of God.

SIN

The Bible is full of descriptions of and instruction concerning the saint's holy war against sinful foes. Metaphors describing the conflict are taken from the scenes and images of war, which was Paul's favorite field of illustration. Our war is against the world, the flesh, and the Devil. This war against sin is one from which there is no discharge. We must remain soldiers until death or until the return of Christ makes possible our demobilization.

Another translation of the phrase "no discharge" in Ecclesiastes 8:8 is "casting off weapons." We can never afford to be off guard. We must not lay aside the weapons of our warfare or loosen our armor for even a moment, because Satan waits to take advantage of the least slackness.

> *Gird thy heavenly armor on,*
> *Wear it ever night and day,*
> *Ambushed lies the evil one,*
> *Watch and pray.*

As each new day dawns we must gird ourselves for the battle. At times we may grow weary in the conflict, but we must wrestle on, for the enemy does not let up. We must appropriate the victory of Calvary in which Jesus by His death and resurrection dealt the enemy of souls His death blow. So we must fight the good fight, for no discharge, no victory, will be ours until the church is saved to sin no more.

SELFISHNESS

Life is a constant battlefield upon which selfishness—individual, social, communal, national—must be daily put to death. Paul speaks vividly of a battle within himself between the "law of God" and the "law of sin," and today we see that the law of greed and selfishness still threatens our home, business, and church. Until our dying day, we will be engaged in a hot contest against all forms of greed. The subtle foe of selfishness dies hard.

If we attack the well fortified enemy of self, whether in our own life or as it appears in the form of evil customs, favorite idols, and victorious lies, we will need the dauntless spirit and the tried nerve of a gallant soldier.

It is very easy to walk on the sunny side of the street, pretending that all is right with the world when our self-importance is being catered to. It is very easy to go through life and never defend the truths the world hates, never defy ridicule, never denounce injustice, never rebuke selfish vices. Heroes are not found among those who take the easy way and who spend their lives hoarding up a little pile and using what they gain upon their own paltry, selfish comforts and mean enjoyments. The selfless Christian does not forget that his first consideration should be how best to serve Christ and advance His cause with what he has.

True soldiers, then, are never discharged from the war against all forms of selfishness. They are daily victorious by the keeping power of God. They follow the selfless example of Christ who did not avoid the agonies of Gethsemane nor the pain of Calvary, but gave of Himself—even unto death—that we might be victorious over our sinfulness.

LIFE'S CARES

One translation of Solomon's phrase says, "In war there is no furlough." How true this is when we come to the cares and responsibilities of life! The firing never ceases in this battle. Day after day we have to endure a great fight of afflictions. The battle goes on until we are taken out of the body in which we work and weep. The great danger of this foe called "life's cares" is that it is made up of little things. No one care is enough to cause us great concern. But taken together, they can catch us unaware and debilitate our spirit. Moreover, because we have so many different concerns, winning the victory over one does not mean we can rest on our laurels. Another care is right behind the first one.

Take the domestic life!

There are multitudes of dear people on whom the burdens and cares of managing a household press heavily. They have only one pair of hands, they cannot do everything, and those around who could help to lift the load are not as thoughtful as they might be.

Are these lines being read by one who feels like giving up and running away? Cheer up! You are serving in the army of the world's bravest fighters. The most significant impact to be made on the world is made in the home. You may think you would like to have no battles in life, to grow on some sheltered plain where the storms never flow and where there are no tears to shed, no loads to carry. But such pampered care never creates robust health.

The heights of blessedness are reached through struggle with disciplining children, serving others, and maintaining a spiritual and loving atmosphere at home. Life's best prizes are for those who graduate from the college of hardship. So, my friend, buckle on the armor again, face the cares of home with the courage of Christ, and your brave spirit will hearten those around more than you realize.

Take the business world!

These are the days of keen competition, elastic business conscience, and sophisticated computer crimes. It is not easy to be honest, sincere, and without reproach. But there is no discharge from the war against every form of trickery, deceit, and underhandedness in the business world. For a soldier of the Lord to decry those tradesmen who use false balances and practice dishonest methods is no simple thing. It may be hard to expose the employer who robs laborers of their hire; to speak out against the rich who grind the poor; to condemn the poor who squander the little they earn on drink, gambling, and soul-destroying pleasures; and at the same time maintain a personal reputation above reproach. Yet having taken the name of Christ, your standard and practice must be characterized by holiness.

Those who try to demonstrate Christian standards of living in the business world have a harder, deadlier fight, requiring more dauntless courage than most others. Resist sloppiness or laxity in business. To be God's person in every phase of business life requires a determination not of earth.

Take the personal realm!

Paul urged Timothy to fight the good fight of faith. If we have enlisted beneath the blood-red banner of our divine captain, then no discharge can be expected in the war against sin and ignorance in our personal lives. To live lives of heroic devotion to God, and to be honest, true, and sincere in the midst of a crooked and perverse generation is the hardest of all tasks and the sternest and longest of all battles. We are to live in chastity, avoiding the slippery paths of sin and the accepted customs of society unworthy of our high calling. We are to live in victory above all the petty things like jealousy, criticism, and unforgiving attitudes, which things we ought to loathe. We are to love the Master with all our heart and never grieve the Holy Spirit by willfully indulging in sin.

Yet, if we fight faithfully under the banner of the cross, when we reach the crystal battlements of heaven, having fought a good fight, we will be found in the army of overcomers. Following the Lamb in His final victory and riding upon white horses, we will be clothed in linen, white and clean. Until the last blow is struck, each of us must play our part. Only cowards run away, leaving braver souls to face the foe. Warring for and with Him who is the absolute commander of our life, let us keep ourselves from those entanglements so disastrous to victory.

TRIALS AND DISAPPOINTMENTS

The sorrows and adversities of life form another foe in the war from which there is no discharge. As good soldiers of Jesus Christ, we are to endure hardness in such a conflict. Trials and disappointments are sometimes the hardest foes to face because they come when our highest expectations are shattered. What we had hoped would go well and easily is marked by frustration. Like his Master, Paul always exemplified his message. He practiced what he preached. Although gentlehearted, he fought against lions and with men fiercer than lions. Closing a career of great trial, suffering, and disappointment, with a voice breaking with tears, the apostle declared that he had fought a good fight.

Perhaps you feel that you are in the hottest part of the battle. Deep wounds are yours, causing bitter pain and anguish. You have been let down by a friend or betrayed by an associate. You wonder when the fighting will stop or when you will receive a furlough from the many trials of life. But, my friend, there is no discharge from the war.

You must be valiant. When armies return from a victorious war, the loudest cheers are not for those who fought the fewest battles or kept their flags the cleanest. Thunderous acclamations are for the regiments cut down to a few men and for the colors riddled with bullets and bloodstained.

It will be the same when we reach heaven, when life's heaviest sufferers will be welcomed to their eternal home of rest. Those who fought the most battles and bore the most marks of the Lord Jesus are to receive the highest honors. The undying attraction of glory are the scars of the Redeemer. Heaven's highest awards will be yours if you suffer patiently and nobly.

SICKNESS AND DISEASE

Thousands of men discharged from a war in which they bravely fought are never discharged from sickness, pain, and injury contracted as the result of war. Think of the hospitals where maimed ex-soldiers are forced to spend their days!

Many there are who put up a brave fight against physical ills. In spite of the astounding victories of science over the ills to which the flesh is heir, what appalling tragedies remain in the physical realm. Cancer and heart attacks are two of the most dreaded foes of health. They stalk the land unchecked and have the best of brains baffled.

Perhaps you are doomed to suffer for the rest of your days. Aches, pains, and infirmities are to be yours until you receive a new body. Seeing that there is no discharge from the war, you must go down to life's last day a happy, resigned warrior, fighting the foe of sickness and disease. You must not bear the brand of a coward. Let it be seen that Satan's servants, who sometimes boast and swagger as if all courage were theirs, are not the only ones who are able to suffer well.

DEATH

The foe of death is, of course, the one Solomon had in mind when he affirmed that there is no dismissal in the war. We can never obtain our discharge in the war against death until death itself gains the mastery. Matthew Henry has said, "The youngest are not released as a fresh soldier nor the oldest as a soldier whose merits have entitled him to a discharge." The death-battle must be fought by each. A substitute is not allowed. No champion can fight for us. But even this last battle holds no dread for those who love the Savior, who "dying, death He slew."

The story is told of a little girl who was being put to bed. "Mommy, must I go to sleep in the dark?" "Yes, my dear, you will be all right. God will be with you, so there is no need to be afraid." But such assurance did not satisfy the timid child, who replied, "I know God will be with me, Mommy, but I should like someone with a *face* to be with me." What a perfectly natural desire of a frightened heart that was!

Yes, amid all the darkness and distress of death, we will need someone near who has a face of cheer and encouragement. We have such a One in the incarnate Christ, whose human face was scarred and marred more than any man's. Therefore let us endure all the battles of life looking only at Him who loved us and gave Himself for us.

Chapter 13

GOD HAS THE BIGGER SHOVEL!

We turn to the subject of stewardship in order to enlighten our conscience, not to issue a stirring appeal to fill the coffers of any church. If only people could be rightly taught concerning stewardship, then it seems to me that the present persistent appeals for money that come in our mailboxes each day and over the airwaves to "maintain the work of the Lord" would be unnecessary.

Somehow there is a widespread misconception regarding the exact nature of stewardship, and we are therefore guilty of a wrong emphasis in our appeals for money. Sometimes people are urged to give who are not truly saved, and if they are saved, they are somewhat carnal and worldly in life. God is not well pleased with the offering of such people. The cause of God is holy, and it uses holy things. Too often we think of stewardship in terms of what we give God as if we are doing Him a favor. In fact, faithful stewardship should be our natural response to God's faithfulness to us as demonstrated by His keeping power.

FAITHFUL STEWARDSHIP IS BIBLICAL

"Moreover it is required in stewards that one be found faithful" (1 Cor. 4:2). First of all, faithful stew-

115

ardship is *biblical*. The term *stewardship* is used in various ways in Scripture. For example, Genesis 15:2 mentions Eliezer, who was a steward of Abraham's household. In that far-off day, a steward was a person whose business it was to provide all the members of the family with food and clothes. This steward received all the cash, spent all that was necessary, and of course kept regular accounts. He was the accountant for a wealthy family.

In Luke 16 is the parable of the unjust steward, in which Christ underscored the term *steward*, for He used that word and its cognates seven times in eight verses. I think the repetition is remarkable because Jesus never wasted words. He was never guilty of tautology. The unjust steward in the parable was commended not because he acted dishonestly, but because he acted wisely for himself. The Lord would have us, as stewards, act wisely and diligently in the use of all that we have.

In 1 Corinthians 4:1, we find the phrase that those who deliver the Word of Life are ". . . Servants of Christ and stewards of the mysteries of God." The mysteries here are the doctrines of grace. They form the divine treasure entrusted to preachers and teachers, a treasure they must guard.

In Titus 1:7 Paul says that a bishop, or overseer, as the word really means, must be ". . . blameless, as the steward of God." Here we have a high ideal the Holy Spirit can help us to realize.

We are urged in 1 Peter 4:10 to be ". . . good stewards of the manifold grace of God." This passage implies that whatever gift or endowment we possess must be looked upon as the Lord's property and used for the promotion of His glory.

Emphasized throughout the Word of God is the instruction that the Lord demands the full, complete surrender of all that we have. "Honor the LORD with thy substance, and with the first-fruits of all thine increase: So shall thy barns be filled with plenty, and thy presses shall burst out with new wine" (Prov. 3:9,10). A similar thought is found in Proverbs 11:24,25: "There is that scattereth, and yet increaseth; and there is that withholdeth more than is meet, but it tendeth to poverty. The liberal soul shall be made fat: and he that watereth shall be watered also himself."

In Matthew 6:19,20, we are urged by our Lord not to lay up for ourselves treasures on earth, but to lay up treasures in heaven, and in Luke 6:38, we read, "Give, and it will be given to you. . . ." In Matthew 25 is the parable of talents in which we discover that if we fail to use in a right way what the Lord makes possible, then He will rob us of our stewardship. So faithful stewardship is *biblical*.

FAITHFUL STEWARDSHIP IS COMPREHENSIVE

One cannot study the passages cited without realizing the folly of identifying stewardship with money only. The surrender of our material possessions is a minor phase of the teaching we are considering. Faithful stewardship covers every realm. It includes what we are as well as what we have, and we should surrender our person to God before our possessions.

Within the range of faithful stewardship we should be willing to realize that God has a definite claim upon our life and service, for stewardship covers every relationship of life. Our goods and our gold are secondary. There must be right employment of our time and of our talents, and then the surrender of our treasures. First our *soul*, then our *service*, and then our *silver*.

It is possible to surrender our silver to the Lord and withhold from Him our soul and our service. What is needed is not merely the devotion of our possessions on a vast scale but the unreserved surrender of our life that it might be used in His service. Alas, it is possible in the surrender of our money to attempt to buy off God. For instance, in Acts 8 Simon offered Peter money if he could have the power of the Holy Spirit. Peter's reply leaves no doubt as to the evil expressed in such an attitude: " 'Your money perish with you, because you have thought that the gift of God may be purchased with money!' " (v. 20). There are those who think that by giving their money they can satisfy their conscience, when what disturbs them is the need for a deeper surrender.

A person may be a tither and yet not a "liver," and what is the use of our tithing unless we have a life that is fully dedicated to God? God is the sole owner of all things, and therefore has the right to all. So, beloved, life must be viewed as a perfect whole, and what God demands first of all is the unreserved surrender of our life to Him. This is where I think Frances Ridley Havergal struck a very deep note in that consecration hymn of hers:

> *Take my life, and let it be*
> *Consecrated, Lord, to Thee;*
> *Take my moments and my days,*
> *Let them flow in ceaseless praise.*

The surrender of our life is the basis of all giving. God does not require our silver and our gold and our material possessions if there is not the full surrender of our life to Him; but if He has our life and our moments and our days, then He will have our silver and our gold as well. But no matter what we offer to Him, if we withhold our life, the best we give in material things is useless in influence.

FAITHFUL STEWARDSHIP IS CHRISTLIKE

What a blessed and beautiful trait faithful stewardship was in the character of our Lord. He always practiced what He preached. He did not say to men, "Now you obey these commands of Mine," irrespective of whether He illustrated in His own life the truth that He declared. If Jesus exhorted men to give, then we can depend upon the fact that He led the way in giving. He did not say, " 'Give, and it will be given to you . . .'" (Luke 6:38) without illustrating something of the principle involved in such an exhortation.

This brings us to the truth of His incarnation, which came about through the voluntary surrender of His glory—". . . rich, yet for your sakes He became poor . . ." (2 Cor. 8:9). Jesus gave and gave and gave, until He became bankrupt by love. He did not have money to give. Jesus was the poorest of all.

We are not told that Jesus tithed, and the probability is that He had nothing to tithe. Although He was the possessor of a vast inheritance, He lived on borrowed things from the time of His birth until His cruel death. Coming among men, He did not have a crib of His own when He was born, and Joseph, His foster father, had to borrow a manger. As He moved among men, He was forever dining at another man's table. He could not claim any home as His own. ". . . the Son of Man has nowhere to lay His head" (Matt. 8:20). He rode on the back of a borrowed ass; and when He wanted to emphasize the truth concerning divine sovereignty and needed a penny with which to make clear the truth, He did not have a coin of His own but had to borrow one. When He died, He did not have a grave of His own. His friends had to borrow a tomb in which to bury Him. He had nothing to leave His dear mother but holy memories. He handed her over to John that he might care for her and play the part of a son. So Jesus lived on borrowed things. He had no money to spend, but He had blood to shed and He shed it freely.

Now it may be that you find satisfaction in flinging a few dollars into the offering plate. You listened to an appeal for money, and God burned upon your mind a sense of your own obligation concerning the maintenance of a church or mission group. But it is one thing to throw your dollars on the plate and to part with your substance in that way, and quite a different thing to place yourself upon the altar with gladness and eagerness that God may take you and use you in His own way for His own glory. It is only as you seek to give your own life that you follow in the footsteps of the Master.

FAITHFUL STEWARDSHIP IS APOSTOLIC

Read the Acts of the Apostles and some of the epistles and you will find them filled with examples and teaching of faithful stewardship. There was a dramatic surrender of possessions on the day of Pentecost, when those early Christians ". . . had all things in common, and sold their possessions and goods, and divided them among all, as anyone had need" (Acts 2:44,45). The same truth is found again in the fourth chapter, verse 32, ". . . neither did anyone say that any of the things he possessed was his own. . . ." They realized, as a result of the pentecostal experience, that the lordship of Jesus involved definite stewardship, that the glorified, risen Lord had divine claim upon their lives and their possessions. The two are linked, for not only did those believers have a common pool and make possible the alleviation of need through their surrendered possessions, but with a marvelous abandon they also gave their lives to the Savior. We read that they hazarded their lives for the sake of their faith. Yes, they followed Jesus in His self-imposed poverty.

Think of that remarkable scene in the third chapter of Acts, in which Peter meets a lame man who is begging for alms at the Beautiful Gate. With a look imploring pity he gazes at Peter, expecting a little money. Listen to the reply of Peter, " 'Silver and gold I do not have, but what I do have I give you: In the name of Jesus Christ of Nazareth, rise up and walk' " (Acts 3:6). If you do not have a nickel to give to the work of the Lord, you have a life that God can use which is of greater importance than the surrender of mere material possessions.

The apostle Paul's support was made possible through the faithful stewardship of Christians in Macedonia, in Jerusalem, and in Corinth. Like his Master, Paul was a poor man. What things had been gain to him, he counted loss for Christ's sake. Thus he was dependent upon what others could give for his support.

In his epistles he yearns for the willing surrender of substance not only for his own needs, but for the needs of other Christians as well. In 1 Corinthians 16. he tells the church at Corinth to lay aside a gift so that he may take it to the church in Jerusalem.

The important fact is that the inspiration and basis of all giving is not the need of some particular church or institution or individual. Let that thought sink into your mind. Rather, the basis for all giving is the resurrection of the Lord Jesus. That is made clear from 1 Corinthians 15 and 16. Read this passage, and you will find that Paul gives one of the most remarkable sermons ever preached on the resurrection of the Lord Jesus. Then read right on into chapter 16, which begins, "Now concerning the collection. . . ." It seems as if Paul has come down from talking about the resurrection to talking about the collection. But no, he brings the collection up to the realm of the resurrection and shows that the basis of all giving is the resurrection of the Lord Jesus. He links the surrender of substance to spiritual reality.

A fuller identification with Jesus Christ in His resurrection would result in an outburst of Christian liberality. Unfortunately too many appeals for funds are based on the need of a particular ministry. If we would only be more concerned with leading Christians into a greater understanding of and identification with the resurrection of Jesus Christ, the worldly goods necessary to carry on a ministry would follow.

FAITHFUL STEWARDSHIP IS PRODUCTIVE

God is no man's debtor. Surrender to Him always means the enrichment of the life that gives. You see, whenever we spend our money, we simply change the form of its value. For example, I have in my hand a ten dollar bill. As I pass a book shop I see in the window a book that I would like, a book that I know will profit my mind, and it is marked $10.00. I go in with my ten dollars and ask for that ten dollar book. I spend my money, but I merely change the form of its value.

When we give our money or our lives we change the control of it. When we yield our money to God it becomes His. Anything we give to Him and to His work immediately comes under His control. Let us remember that we are called upon to surrender our substance, not that it might become His but because it is His already. "The silver is mine, and the gold is mine, saith the LORD of hosts" (Hag. 2:8). We give to Him of what we have, because it is His by creation, by redemption, and by every other right.

Faithful stewardship produces the highest dividends and the best interest. In recent years there has been an increasing opportunity to make high rates of return on money invested. It has been possible, for instance, to receive sixteen percent interest on a money-market certificate or eighteen percent on money-market funds. But what is eighteen percent in comparison with what the Lord will give you for your money? What will He give? You shall ". . . receive a hundredfold now in this time . . . and in the age to come, eternal life" (Mark 10:30). So as you can see, faithful stewardship yields high dividends.

Moreover, investment in the cause of Christ represents absolute security. No thieves can ever carry off what you give to God, and inflation cannot have any effect whatever upon your investments in the things belonging to the kingdom. Faithful stewardship produces joy, for giving always rebounds in blessing. Good givers are always happy souls.

Furthermore, faithful stewardship produces eternal rewards. "'Who then is that faithful and wise steward, whom his master will make ruler over his household . . . ?'" (Luke 12:42). What do we know about laying up treasures in heaven? God does not want to deprive us of our possessions. He desires us to send them on before. What do we know about laying up treasures in heaven, investing our money in those ways that help to perpetuate our influence? Will you invest your possessions in lives and in churches and in those institutions that make for the furtherance of the cause of the Lord Jesus among men? May God give us grace to convert our cash into character.

The story is told of a good farmer who loved the Lord and believed in stewardship. He was very generous. His friends asked him how he could give so much and yet remain prosperous. "We cannot understand you," his friends said. "Why, you seem to give more than the rest of us and yet you always seem to have greater prosperity."

"Oh," said the farmer, "that is very easy to explain. You see I keep shoveling into God's bin and God keeps shoveling more and more into mine, and *God has the bigger shovel.*"

Will you remember that? God has the bigger shovel. We are so selfish about surrendering all that we are and have, we forget that the Lord is no man's debtor. We never give without receiving; surrender always means enrichment. God has the bigger shovel, and when we are generous in our giving, God is generous in what He gives back to us. And so we come back to the wonderful words of Jesus, "Give, and it will be given to you: good measure, pressed down, shaken together, and running over will be put into your bosom" (Luke 6:38).

Our true motive for faithful stewardship, however, must not be that we will get more back from God. Rather it should always be a grateful response to God's faithfulness to us as demonstrated by His keeping power.

Chapter 14

ARE YOU A GOOD HATER?

Almost ninety years ago, Britain was deeply moved by William Ewart Gladstone, a former prime minister who, well over eighty years of age and nearly blind, emerged from his retirement to utter protest against the horrible massacre of the Armenians by the Turks. There were those selfish, shallow persons who sneeringly said of Gladstone, "Fanatical old man! Better have stuck to his fireside and his Homer." But by his fearless and courageous condemnation of such horrible slaughter, he kept the nation's soul alive.

Samuel Johnson said of a friend, "He is a good hater." The psalmist who wrote, "You who love the LORD, hate evil!" (Ps. 97:10), was certainly a good hater with an intense hatred for all that was alien to God's holy mind and will.

Why is it in our day that even where the Bible is believed and preached people have toned down their vocal disapproval of sin? If the church were once again filled with haters of evil, power would be hers to blister the conscience of any nation in which she is found. In one of his essays, Lord Morley, writing of Emerson's easy optimism said, "In like manner Emerson has little to say of that horrid burden and impediment on the soul which the churches call *sin*, and which, by whatever name we call it, is a very real catastrophe in the moral nature of man."

As Christians, do we have the burning hate and passionate antagonism toward every monstrous, loathsome form of sin, so evident in the "horrid burden and impediment" of earth's millions? Do we share the apostolic abhorrence of idolatry and evil? (see Rom. 2:22; 12:9). Has the naked truth dawned upon our minds that if we cannot be angry and yet sin not, we cannot be holy?

HOLY HATRED, DIVINE LOVE

If we do not hate evil as God does, then we do not love as He loves. There is a holy hatred, and the measure of our hostility against "the very real catastrophe in the moral nature of man" is the measure of our passion for all that is true and noble. These opposite passions complement each other and form a single white passion of divine love in the soul, which, like a rushing mountain torrent as the snows melt, sweeps away all obstacles and submerges the black rocks that lie in its path.

If the world is to be brought face to face with the holiness of God, hatred of sin must be the temper of all the saints. We dare not allow ourselves to have an easy toleration of vice, but we should maintain an unceasing and fiery hostility against all that insults the majesty and holiness of heaven. It is said that one day a rogue called at the Eversley Rectory where Charles Kingsley lived. Opening the door, Kingsley saw the man on his knees, turning up the whites of his eyes, and uttering a disgusting counterfeit of prayer. Holy anger came upon

Kingsley, who was known as one of the most tender-hearted of men. Seizing the hypocrite by the wrist and coat collar, he threw him toward the garden gate.

Kingsley and others like him—John the Baptist, Luther, Latimer, and John Knox to name a few—were worthy followers of the Lord Jesus Christ, who, eyes flashing with indignation and anger, took the whip and drove the impious merchants out of God's Temple. Are we following in their footsteps as stouthearted protestors against all that is evil and crooked, whether it is found in business, in government, or among individuals? We may never have the privilege of being numbered among those heroic Christian knights who fearlessly denounced the wickedness of courts, kings, and nations and who only courted ostracism and death as their reward, but by God's grace we can rebuke the works of darkness that occur among our friends and acquaintances. There are two thoughts to bear in mind concerning holy hatred.

To hate evil is to be Christ-like

The righteousness of Jehovah flows through the Bible as a turbulent, purifying river, bearing away the foulnesses and falsities of men and nations. Everywhere the divine Voice is raised against abominable practices and persons. As an anonymous writer of nearly a century ago expressed it,

> The Old Testament presents a long catalogue of abominations against which God has declared a war of extermination—the froward mouth, lying lips, the proud look, the false ways and oaths, vain thoughts,

corrupt imaginations, serving other gods, jealousy of others, unkindness to neighbors, vain oblations, paraded prayers, fasting and alms, negligence of widows and orphans, unclean altars, sanctuaries of hypocrisy, the substitution of ritual for righteousness, the lusting after idolatries, riches and sensualities, and every other corrupt and satanic work.

The goodness of God should never be magnified at the expense of His severity. If only good, winking His eye at evil, He would be unrighteous; if only severe, with no mercy for repentant offenders, He would be brutal. But Scripture teaches that, with God, goodness and severity are in harmony. God is love, yet He is a consuming fire. Do we not pale before the scathing words and denunciations of the "Gentle Jesus, meek and mild" when He confronted His religious antagonists? Think of His eightfold woe (see Matt. 23), and you will realize that He was no weak amiable Deity indifferent to moral distinctions, but One who could both love and hate. As Dale of Birmingham once wrote, "The words of Christ, uttered with anger and indignation, as He confronted the ungodliness and unrighteousness of men, are words which shake the heart with fear." Do we emulate Christ's passion against wickedness? Henry Drummond felt such passion when, trying to cleanse student life in Edinburgh, he cried out, "Oh, I am sick with the sins of these men! How can God bear it?"

To live near the heart of God can be a costly matter, especially when, with His eyes, we see the streets of earth so often knee-deep in moral mire and filth. Before God's holy wrath crushes the rebellions and devilries of man, we must strive to deliver sinners from their evil ways.

Are You A Good Hater?

To hate evil is the method to make the world God-like

John Wesley once declared, "Give me a hundred men who hate nothing but sin and fear nothing but God, and I will turn the world upside down." And it was no vain boast! Wesley's preachers became the spiritual scavengers of their century. Theirs was no shallow humanitarianism impotent to heal and lift a corrupt world. They wielded the sword of the Spirit and slew dreaded giants of their time. Sin haters, they became men-savers. Today, corruption prevails in every phase of society and if ours is to be an effective Christian abhorrence of all evil, we must keep before us a few guiding principles.

First of all, we must distinguish between sin and sinners. The eloquent truth of the Bible is that God loves sinners but hates their sins. Certainly He is angry with evildoers and not with mere abstractions. But He only manifests His wrath against people who allow themselves to become incarnations of wickedness, embodiments of injustice, seduction, unrighteousness, and all ungodliness. It is therefore only because they deliberately choose to become the vehicle, the mouthpiece, the expression of sin that they earn divine condemnation. God's fiercest hatred, however, is against sin itself.

Moreover, a holy hater is always slow to accuse others and excuse himself. Those who serve God best are most conscious of their own sinfulness and shortcomings. One day a missionary companion admiringly said to Mary Slessor of Calabar that she was not worthy to tie Mary's shoe. Mary replied, "Dear daughter of the King, why do you say that? If you knew me as God does, you would not have said a thing like that." We defeat God's purpose in rebuking evil-workers if we adopt a holier-than-thou attitude. The holy hater will always be most severe with himself. He will always be relentless in dealing with the plague of his own heart.

Our concluding observation is that holy haters are never vindictive. Their wrath, like that of the Lord's, is always redemptive. In wrath there is the remembrance of mercy. Although our abhorrence of evil is to be a vehement, white-hot passion constraining one to combat iniquity no matter where found, we must have an eagerness to convert, not condemn, those caught in the whirlpool of sin.

Genuine haters of evil are one of the greatest needs of the contemporary church. The world needs a courageous army which is not afraid to rebuke the Devil. We should pray that in these critical days when a veritable tornado of wicked and murderous hate is sweeping over the world, blasting all divine qualities God meant man to manifest, possibly ending in a nuclear war of annihilation, that God Himself would raise up a mighty host in His church who, without fear or favor, are prepared to witness as stouthearted protestors of all that is alien to God's righteous will and purpose.

Chapter 15

KEPT FOR THE KINGDOM

The airplane has certainly revolutionized our method of traveling between cities and countries. Because I am ninety-five years of age, I can remember when in England, my birthplace, there were no planes, no automobiles, no buses, no fast seagoing vessels. Travel was simple and slow, for apart from walking we had to rely on horse-drawn vehicles, bicycles, and trains.

On my first visit to America almost fifty years ago, the only means of covering the long distance from London to Chicago was by ship from Southampton to New York, taking almost six days at that time, and then by train to Chicago. But when I returned to London a few years ago on the initial flight of the Concorde, the distance of nearly 4,000 miles from Washington to London took only three hours and twenty-five minutes. What enormous speed!

But even the tremendous speed of the Concorde will seem to be nothing when all the saints are caught up in a moment, even before they can wink the eye, to meet the Lord in the air. We will then cover the immeasurable distance from earth to heaven in a flash. Since God is, by His power, keeping us for His eternal kingdom, let us devote this closing chapter to the return of our Lord.

Our Lord's return ought to lead us into a richer devotion to Him whose glory is the culmination of prophecy—God's beloved Son and our Savior, Jesus Christ. Furthermore, we have the confidence that the numerous prophecies concerning Him that are already fulfilled are the guarantee that all the predictions as to His future appearance and activities will also be fulfilled. "I have spoken it, I will also bring it to pass; I have purposed it, I will also do it" (Is. 46:11). May our personal understanding of all that the coming days hold both for Christ and ourselves result in a life that is holy and filled with an eager expectancy!

While the term "Second Advent," as well as that of "First Advent," is not to be found in Scripture, everything that such terms imply flood its sacred pages. The word *Trinity* is not in the Bible either, but the fact is everywhere proclaimed. We are distinctly told that Christ is coming *the second time* (see Heb. 9:28). What else can this phrase mean but His Second Advent, since *advent* means "coming"? In fact the three distinct appearings of Jesus are brought together in the ninth chapter of Hebrews:

". . . now, once . . . He has appeared to put away sin by the sacrifice of Himself" (Heb. 9:26)—PAST

"Christ . . . entered . . . into heaven itself, now to appear in the presence of God for us" (Heb. 9:24)—PRESENT

"Christ . . . will appear a second time . . ." (Heb. 9:28)—FUTURE

The *backward* look, the *upward* look, and the *forward* look offer a complete revelation of our Savior. What a great

loss is ours if we emphasize only those aspects of
Christ's life that we can look at historically and neglect
the *forward* look, striving, thereby, to live without hope.
Dr. J. G. Simpson in his great work *Christus Crucifixus*
says,

> There are abundant indications that the confidence
> with which the author of The Epistle to the Hebrews
> looked forward to the return of the Great High Priest,
> who had passed into the sanctuary of the heavens,
> was shared by multitudes of believing men for many
> generations, inspiring the hope of confessors, sus-
> taining the faith of martyrs, establishing the patience
> of saints. . . . In times of stress, when the winds and
> waves have roared and hearts have failed for fear,
> God's saints have been upheld by the vision of the
> Son of Man sitting at the right hand of power and
> coming in the clouds. The joy of the thought of His
> return turned the lonely Aegean rocks and the dark
> Roman catacomb into the ante-chamber of heaven
> itself.

May we experience such a "blessed hope." Christ's
second coming is no idle theory or vain though beautiful vision with no possible practical result. Rather, it is
an aspect of divine truth kindling our energies into
flame, banishing all lifeless inactivity! The whole of life
will be ennobled if we live in the light of the constant
expectation of Christ's return.

It is said that on one occasion during a session of the
U.S. Senate, a sudden and very dense darkness fell
upon Washington. So awful, so intense did this become
that the probability of the end of the world was freely
discussed, and one of the senators moved for an immediate adjournment. But another well-known mem-

ber rose to his feet and in reply to the proposal said, "I propose that lights be brought in and that we proceed with our business. If the Judge come, He had better find us at our duty." Surely this sentiment should motivate all who believe that Christ is coming again. "Blessed is that servant whom his master, when he comes, will find so doing" (Matt. 24:46).

The term "the Second Advent" is a general one covering many events that are associated with our Lord from the time of His return for His church until the end of the Millennium. We must distinguish between two specific events or stages of His coming. When the hour arrives for Jesus to leave heaven to fulfill His own promise, "I will come again," He will not descend to earth without a break. On the way down He is to pause in the air for a most stupendous event, and then after a while continue His coming to the world. Scripture suggests that there will be certain events occurring between the two stages of His one coming. We will be confused if we fail to observe these two phases: ". . . to meet the Lord *in the air* . . ." (1 Thess. 4:17, italics added) and "His feet shall stand . . . . *upon the mount of Olives* . . ." (Zech. 14:4, italics added).

The first event is that His true church will be raptured to meet Him in the heavenlies, or somewhere between earth and heaven. After the judgment of the saints and their preparation to rule with Christ on earth comes the second event, which is connected with His millennial reign. Paul reminds us that the saints are to reign with Him, and it therefore seems likely that after coming for His saints and gathering them around Him, Christ will bring them back to earth when the time comes to assist Him in the governmental control of all things here below.

A scholar of the last century drew an analogy between Christ's return and the return of Charles II of England from his exile. In this historical event there were two distinct stages. During the first stage the king's loyal and devoted adherents who had been true to him through the time of the Commonwealth under Cromwell went across the Channel to meet him in France. Charles met with them, and they discussed the plans for their campaign to take back England. All the details of Charles's return were settled at this stage. The second stage came when Charles, with his company of loyal adherents, crossed the sea, landed in England, and was revealed to the nation as the returning king.

Then there followed his enthronement as the sovereign, the trial and judgment of the leading rebels, and the undisputed reign of Charles over the whole land. Apart from the character of Charles II, the two aspects of his return closely resemble the gathering of saints to the returning heavenly king, and afterwards His manifestation as King of kings to the whole world.

Among the several words used to describe the coming again of Christ, we have these three conspicuous ones, all of which imply that He will be personally present with those who participate in the event.

Parousia, indicating presence, arrival—"the being or becoming present." In Matthew we read, "So also will the coming [*parousia*] of the Son of Man be" (Matt. 24:27,39). He who was not formerly seen will now be visible.

Apokalupsis, meaning "revelation," "unveiling," "exposure to view" (see Luke 17:30; 1 Pet. 4:13). This word is from *apokalupto*, which means "to take off the cover," from which we get the word Apocalypse, the term used to describe the Book of Revelation.

Epiphancia implies "appearing" or "bringing forth into light," "causing to shine," and assures us that Christ will naturally appear and be manifested in a visible way (see 1 Tim. 6:14; 2 Tim. 4:8). We are to see Him as He is, and such a disclosure will be accompanied by His shining glory. Our Lord will shine (*epiphancia*) upon those brought into His presence (*parousia*).

HE PROMISED TO RETURN FOR HIS CHURCH

While He was with His disciples, Jesus said, "I will send my Spirit" (see John 16:7). He fulfilled this promise when the Holy Spirit came upon the believers on the day of Pentecost. Jesus also said, "I will build my church (see Matt. 16:18). He fulfilled this promise also, for there is not a country on the face of the earth that has not felt the impact of the church of Jesus Christ. It is His third promise that we are now considering: "I will come again" (see John 14:3). Just as He fulfilled His first two promises, so we can expect Him to fulfill His third.

This third promise was made when Jesus was gathered with His eleven apostles in the Passover chamber. Judas was missing from the company, having gone out to complete the arrangements of the betrayal of His master. A deep gloom rested upon the small assembly because Jesus had told them that He was about to leave them. " '. . . Where I am going you cannot follow Me now . . .' " (John 13:36). Then He uttered some of the most sublime words ever to leave His holy lips. Jesus revealed to His distressed friends the secret of an untroubled heart:

Faith in Himself—". . . believe also in Me."

Faith in heaven—"In My Father's house are many dwelling places. . . ."

Faith in His return—". . . I will come again . . ." (see John 14:1–3).

Later on Jesus, linking His death, resurrection, and second advent together, gave His disciples the comforting hope, ". . . I will see you again and your heart will rejoice . . ." (John 16:22). What must be borne in mind is the fact that He was speaking to His own, as He called the disciples. As such they represented His church in its entirety, for when He said, ". . . I will . . . receive you to Myself . . ." (John 14:3), He did not imply only the eleven men around Him, but the multitudes all through the ages who would believe in Him, of whom the disciples were forerunners. The assurance of His coming is repeated, ". . . 'You have heard how I said to you, "I am going away and coming back to you" . . .' " (John 14:28). This assurance is a particular promise for a particular people. It is given only to those who have come to the Father through the Son, for Jesus said, ". . . 'I am the way, the truth, and the life . . .' " (John 14:6).

There are those who belittle any thought of a personal return of Christ, but language has no meaning if He is not coming as He said He would. ". . . I will come again. . . ." Because of all He is in Himself, He must return. If He does not, then He is a liar and not *The Truth* as He declares Himself to be. ". . . Hath he spoken, and shall he not make it good?" (Num. 23:19). We are to look for the man who left us a promise to return, and we know that we shall not be disappointed.

If this were the only place in the New Testament where this first event of the Second Advent is mentioned, it would be sufficient for faith to lean upon, seeing it is a divine promise. But there follow many ratifications of the promise. For instance, as soon as Jesus entered heaven, two glorified men left heaven to confirm His declaration. They said, ". . . This same Jesus, who was taken up from you into heaven, will so come in like manner as you have seen Him go into heaven" (Acts 1:11).

He went away in the presence of His own, and He will return in like manner. In unmistakable language, Paul enlarges upon the promise of His coming, declaring that the church is to gather around the Lord in the air (see 1 Thess. 4:13–18). Peter tells us that the Lord will not be slack concerning the fulfillment of His promise (2 Pet. 3:9). From Hebrews we learn that Christ is to appear "the second time" and that, " '. . . He who is coming will come and will not tarry' " (Heb. 9:28; 10:37).

The last recorded words of Jesus reiterate His promise given in the upper chamber, "Surely I am coming quickly" (Rev. 22:20). No wonder John gave as the last prayer of the Bible a yearning for His return, "Even so, come, Lord Jesus" (Rev. 22:20).

SHALL WE KNOW EACH OTHER IN HEAVEN?

A friend asked George Macdonald, the Scottish novelist and poet, "Shall we know one another in heaven?" His pointed reply was, "Shall we be greater fools in paradise than we are here?" Consciousness, fellowship, love, memory, personal identity involve recognition. Each individual will possess hereafter a recognizable personality and faculties superior to those exercised on earth. We may not recognize each other in the same way we do now, but there is no doubt that we will know each other. Paul reminds us that heaven is the home of ". . . the whole family in heaven and earth . . ." (Eph. 3:15). What kind of a home would it be if its members are to be strangers to each other forever? We can assume with certainty that we shall know one another more thoroughly in the life beyond. ". . . Then I shall know just as I also am known" (1 Cor. 13:12). Heaven means a more holy, blessed intimacy, which our present human frailties prevent.

> *We shall know each other better*
> *When the mists have rolled away.*

This agelong, passionate desire to know each other better has a strong sentimental value and is a perfectly legitimate one. Heaven will not be heaven if it does not offer reunion with and the recognition of our dead in Christ. All love is of God, John reminds us, and because such love cannot be buried in a coffin, the beautiful but broken relationships of earth are resumed in the Father's home above where, as members of the same family, we will dwell together in perfect harmony.

The Bible offers sufficient evidence of recognition among the occupants of heaven. We can be perfectly sure that the angels around the throne of God know one another. They praise God together and carry out His will together. Surely, the two angels found sitting at the Savior's tomb and who announced His resurrection recognized one another!

Jesus spoke about sitting down with Abraham, Isaac, and Jacob in heaven. How could he do this without recognizing them? What kind of a fellowship could there be if these patriarchs did not retain their identity?

(see Matt. 8:11). David, as he wept over his dead child, knew that he would join him again at death. ". . . I shall go to him . . ." (2 Sam. 12:23). Remember, David had only seen the baby Bathsheba had borne him for a few days, yet he believed he would distinguish their baby from the millions in heaven. David looked beyond the vast universe to the place of reunion, saying, "My child is there. I shall go to him."

Two men came down from the glory land to have a conversation with Jesus about His death at Jerusalem. Jesus had taken three of His disciples, Peter, James, and John, to the summit of a mountain, and while there the two heavenly visitants appeared: Moses who lived at approximately 1350 B.C. and Elijah at 870 B.C. (see Matt. 17:1–8). Peter, of course, had never seen these Old Testament saints in the flesh, yet he immediately recognized them, for he said, "Let us make here three tabernacles: one for You, one for Moses, and one for Elijah." Thus their identity must have been obvious.

The rich man in hell recognized both Abraham and Lazarus (see Luke 16:19–31). Although there is much mystery surrounding the parable, this much is evident: there was unmistakable recognition. Identity had not been destroyed.

In His resurrected body, Jesus retained His identity. In the twilight Mary supposed Jesus to be the gardener. He clearly appeared as a human being. But as soon as He spoke, Mary recognized the voice—the same voice that had previously spoken to her soul. The two disciples on the road to Emmaus did not recognize Jesus for the special reason Luke explains, "Their eyes were restrained, so that they did not know Him" (Luke 24:16). But later at supper, as He broke bread, the film fell from their eyes, and they instantly recognized Him (see Luke 24:31).

Will the righteous be able to converse with the Lord in heaven? Surely if we can speak to Him now in prayer we shall be able to do so more perfectly over there. How could we be "at home" with Him and not recognize Him and be recognized by Him? "Social fellowship, so far from ceasing in heaven, will be vastly extended, and each of us will know intuitively the whole family of God. What a gathering of the ransomed that will be." If you have a dear one in heaven whom your heart yearns to see, do not despair, for you will meet again. The voice you loved to hear, you will hear again. The identity of the one you were near to on earth remains the same, and instant recognition will be yours as you meet never to part again. Your beloved one is only lost a little while.

One of the great thrills in heaven will be not only meeting our dear ones again, but meeting the great saints of the ages. Abraham, Moses, David, Paul, all the rest of the prophets and apostles, and the martyrs and the divines of the centuries. As we meet them on the golden streets, we will be able to talk with them as long as we want to. As children of the same family, and all in heaven through the grace of God, introductions will be unnecessary, as we shall all meet on the common ground of relationship. The poet asks—

> *Shall we know the friends that greet us*
> *In that glorious spirit land?*
> *Shall we see the same eyes shining*
> *On us as in the days of yore?*

The Keeping Power of God

Shall we feel the dear arms twining
Fondly round us as before?

Cardinal Newman in "Lead, Kindly Light" answers the question:

And with the morn those angel faces smile,
Which I have loved long since, and lost awhile.

ALL OF THIS AND MORE

We've talked of our Lord's return, our own resurrection and bodily transformation "in the twinkling of an eye," and that glorious reunion with those of "like precious faith" whom we will know and recognize. But space prohibits us from speaking of the glorious city, the myriad of angels, the river, and the tree of life. Our words cannot express the radiance of glory that awaits those who are kept by the power of God.

Immediately following the promise of God's keeping power, the apostle Peter exhorts us,

In this you greatly rejoice, though now for a little while, if need be, you have been grieved by manifold temptations, that the genuineness of your faith, being more precious than gold that perishes, though it is tested with fire, may be found to praise, honor, and glory at the revelation of Jesus Christ (1 Pet. 1:6,7).

125401